BACKYARD BIRDS

of the

INLAND EMPIRE

BACKYARD BIRDS

of the

INLAND EMPIRE

SHEILA N. KEE

Heyday Books, Berkeley, California
Riverside-Corona Resource Conservation District

This book was made possible in part by a generous grant from the James Irvine Foundation.

Library of Congress Cataloging-in-Publication Data

Kee, Sheila N.
  Backyard birds of the Inland Empire / Sheila N. Kee.
    p. cm.
  Includes bibliographical references and index.
  ISBN 978-1-59714-132-1 (pbk. : alk. paper)
  1. Bird watching—Inland Empire (Pacific Northwest) 2. Birds—Inland Empire (Pacific Northwest)—Identification. I. Title.
  QL683.P36K44 2010
  598.072'34795—dc22   2009039734

Cover Art: Female house finch by Oskar F. Neuhold,
  courtesy of the photographer
Cover Design: Lorraine Rath
Interior Design/Typesetting: Leigh McLellan Design
Printing and Binding: Printed in China by Everbest Printing Co.
  through Four Colour Imports, Ltd., Louisville, Kentucky

Orders, inquiries, and correspondence
should be addressed to:
  Heyday Books
  P. O. Box 9145, Berkeley, CA 94709
  (510) 549-3564, Fax (510) 549-1889
  www.heydaybooks.com

10 9 8 7 6 5 4 3 2 1

CONTENTS

SPECIES DESCRIPTIONS
ARRANGED BY CONSPICUOUS COLOR

Descriptions of birds marked with an asterisk (*) are found on the male's species page.

**Description found on the page of the most common coloration.

APPENDICES

ACKNOWLEDGMENTS

I would like to thank the Riverside-Corona Resource Conservation District's Board of Directors and Shelli Lamb, District Manager, for giving me the opportunity to make my dream a reality.

A big thanks to Diana Ruiz, Public Affairs Manager for the Riverside-Corona Resource Conservation District, for the long hours spent helping to edit the book and lay out the original publication.

I would like to express my heartfelt thanks to Tracy Tennant, Jean Weiss, Bill Gary, Katie Shea, Nanette Pratini, Chet McGaugh, and Tom Scott for taking time out of their busy schedules to review this book for me. Their excellent comments have helped to make it more readable. Thanks also for initial input from Andy Sanders. Sylvia Gallagher, from Sea and Sage Audubon, was a tremendous help in the beginning stages of the book and in helping me choose just the right photos to use. I'm indebted to all those who provided pictures, especially James Gallagher, who provided most of the photos for this book.

A thank-you goes to Dr. Edith Allen, Cooperative Extension Specialist at the University of California, Riverside, for her continued support as I attempted to follow some of my dreams.

I deeply appreciate the supportive and patient staff at Heyday and publisher Malcolm Margolin for taking this book to an enhanced, second edition and for enlisting the help of the James Irvine Foundation and the Inlandia Institute.

A special thank-you to my husband, Stu Hemstreet, for all his encouragement during the writing process. It would have been much less fun and exciting without his feedback. And I thank him also for all those breakfasts he provided me while I worked at home!

All unlabeled photos are by photographer James Gallagher.

To my mother and father,
who taught me the joy and beauty of nature.

—Sheila Kee

The Riverside-Corona Resource Conservation District (RCRCD) commissioned Sheila Kee to create this guide to share her passion for the birds of the Inland Empire, specifically the inland valleys of western Riverside and San Bernardino Counties, in southern California. In 2002, the first edition was self-published by RCRCD as a tool for learning about one essential component of this unique place: birds.

Our goals today remain the same as then. Therefore, we present this beautiful, updated version:

- To raise awareness about natural resources—in this case, local birds;

- To provide information about creating sustainable yards that are bird-friendly: stepping-stones of habitat from wildlands into cities;

- To foster natural pest control methods (some kinds of birds devour insects);

- To support pollinators and their important role in facilitating the production of food and fiber; and

- To provide tools for greening the urban ecosystem into something that performs more like a natural ecosystem. Nature's systems filter and store water, clean air, regenerate fertile soils, regulate flooding, contribute to climate stability, and much more.

Enjoy the birds! Not only are they fun and interesting to watch, they play an important role in our ecosystems.

GETTING STARTED

Cactus wren nest, found at Mt. Rubidoux

Photo by Sheila Kee

Introduction

Did you ever see a "little brown bird" in your yard and wonder what it was? But when you looked in the bird books, you couldn't find it? If so, then this book is for you.

I decided to write this book because when my non-birder friends and coworkers get frustrated with the bird books, they come to me to help them identify their mystery bird. After asking them enough questions, I can usually identify the bird. They are amazed! But here's my secret: of the hundreds of bird species in the United States, only a relatively small number would occur commonly in your yard in the Inland Empire.

My hope is to increase your understanding and enjoyment of what exists in your own backyard and neighborhood. For example, my next-door neighbor, knowing nothing of birds, was upset when a Nuttall's Woodpecker landed on her sycamore tree and began to pick off the bark. She had just raked her yard and did not want any more debris falling into it. When I explained that the woodpecker was actually doing her a favor by removing insects that could damage her tree, thereby helping the tree to stay healthy, she decided that she did not mind the mess after all.

When you start noticing the birds in your own yard, all of a sudden you realize they are all around you. In the midst of our personal day-to-day activities, they, too, are carrying on their lives, raising their families, singing, catching dinner and eating it, and, sometimes, squabbling.

I wanted to share with you, from one urban dweller to another, the joy that comes from knowing nature more intimately. What better way to learn to appreciate the planet we all share than to learn about our bird "neighbors"? My main hope is that you can slow down from your busy routine, just for a little while, and enjoy the unfolding drama going on around you. But be forewarned, it *is* addicting!

How to Use This Book

There are approximately fifty bird species that are common in the Inland Empire, birds that you could expect to find in your yard. Familiarize yourself with them by looking through the *Species Descriptions* section.

Color and size are the characteristics of a bird that you are most likely to notice. Thus, I have organized the *Species Descriptions* section by color, as an easy reference and starting point. But a word of caution: I have organized the birds into chapters by the color of the male. If the male and female look alike, great! But, if you can't find the species description for a bird in what seems to be the appropriate color category, it may be a female or an immature bird. For example, the Hooded Oriole is placed in the "Black and Orange" color category, because of the male's color. However, the female is yellow. You will find her listed in the table of contents under "Yellow Accents," but her species description is in the "Black and Orange" chapter.

I have included as much basic information about each bird as I thought would be interesting, hopefully without being overwhelming. This includes brief discussions of where and when the bird is most likely to be seen, what the bird looks like (both adults and immatures), and what species are similar or easily confused. The *Glossary* at the back of the book will help with unfamiliar terms.

I have provided lists of the Inland Empire's most common birds, arranged by different characteristics: what time of year you are likely to see them, their size, their behavior, group/family traits, and food preference. Comparing these lists will help you identify the birds you see. Often, color will be the first thing you notice, but you may also notice where a bird is feeding, for example. Thus, by comparing the list of *Birds by Behavior* and the *Table of Contents*, where the birds are listed by color, you will be able to narrow down your choices.

Photos of each unique bird are provided in the *Species Descriptions*. I've included photos of the male and female, if they are significantly different. I've also provided photos of males in breeding and nonbreeding plumage, if it differs. Immatures are included if they differ significantly from adults.

The small sections under the photographs, called "*Key Things to Look For,*" list the most basic things to observe quickly in order to identify a bird and distinguish it from other similar ones. If you answer yes to all (or most) of the points, you probably have identified the bird!

For the most confusing birds (often the females and immatures), I have developed a section called *Look-alikes* so you can see the similar photos side by side.

This book is not meant to be a replacement for a field guide, but is rather an aid to help you ID and learn the birds that are likely to be around you. However, I also make reference to birds that occur here only rarely or irregularly. I suggest that you eventually learn what they look like, just in case you happen to have one in your yard. There was not room to include details about every potential rare or unusual bird, but I did include a list, *Unusual Birds You Might See in Your Yard.* This list will help you narrow down what to look for in a field guide.

When you refer to a field guide, you will notice that it is not set up like this book. Birds are not usually organized by color. Instead they are classified by an established taxonomy, arranged in order from the most ancient to the most recently evolved families and species. Field guides developed for the United States begin with the loons, considered the oldest living bird species, and end with the sparrows, considered the youngest living bird species that occurs in the U.S.

A family of birds is a group that shares common structural characteristics. Some families have hundreds of species, and others have only one. Learning basic family characteristics will be very useful in determining what type of bird you are looking at. And I strongly suggest you do so. See the list *Birds by Group.*

I urge you to use this book over and over, until it becomes worn from use. Don't even bother putting it on a shelf. Just leave it out in a convenient place for continual reference. Remember, the birds will be just outside your windows, every day.

Please, read all the introductory information. It really will help you understand the basics about birds and birding.

And, most of all, *have fun!*

Location, Location, Location

Where you live will influence what birds you actually see. For example, if you live along the coast, you will tend to see different birds than if you live on the edge of a desert.

The species and numbers of birds you see will differ if you live on five acres of open space or in a high-density neighborhood with little vegetation. If you live close to a large open space, such as the Box Springs Mountains, Sycamore Canyon, a large campus, a golf course, or along the Santa Ana River, you will see more species.

In addition, what birds you see will depend on whether you provide such things as water, feeding stations, and nesting sites, and whether you or your neighbors have cats. See the Appendix C, *Attracting Birds to Your Yard,* for more information about enhancing backyard habitat.

Tools

1. **This book.**

2. **Binoculars.** For the most enjoyment, invest in a decent pair of binoculars. Binoculars will allow you to observe bird behavior, color, and detail. Refer to bird magazines for articles that can help you find the best pair of binoculars for your needs and budget.

 Binoculars can be frustrating when you're first learning to use them. And it doesn't help that birds seem to sit just long enough for you to get your binoculars up and then fly away!

 After you've spotted a bird, continue to follow it with your naked eye as you move the binoculars up to your eyes. If you can't find the bird, lower the binoculars slightly, until you sight the bird again. Then raise the binoculars. Don't try to search for the bird through the binoculars. And, have patience. You'll get the hang of it with practice.

3. **Field guides.** There are so many bird identification books available that it is difficult to recommend any specific one. *But do get one!* If you can only get one, select a guide that focuses on the western United States, not just a localized area.

One of the very best beginning birder's books is *Birds of North America: A Guide to Field Identification,* an illustrated guide by Chandler S. Robbins (St. Martin's Press Golden Field Guides, 2001). Roger Tory Peterson's *Field Guide to Western Birds* (Houghton Mifflin Harcourt, 1998) uses arrows to indicate what specific field marks to look for when identifying a bird. If you prefer photographs to illustrations, you might like the *Stokes Field Guide to Birds: Western Region* by Donald and Lillian Stokes (Little, Brown, 1994). National Geographic and National Audubon Society have excellent field guides; however, beginning birders may find them a little intimidating. See *References and Suggested Reading* for more information.

Top Ten Points for Beginners to Know

One: Songs vs. calls. Male birds are the only ones that sing, with a few notable exceptions. In the Inland Empire, the females that sing include the House Finch, Northern Mockingbird, Bullock's Oriole, and Black-headed Grosbeak. Birds usually sing only in breeding season. *Listen* and notice how noisy it gets in the springtime, during the height of breeding season, and how quiet it is in the late summer. Both females and males have calls that are used all year long to maintain their bonds, defend their territories, or keep in contact as they forage for food. Songs tend to be much more intricate and elaborate than calls, which are often just one note.

Two: Coloration. The males usually have the most colorful feathers. In some species, however, such as the Mockingbird or Scrub Jay, it is virtually impossible for us humans to tell the male and female apart. (Somehow, they can!) Some species, such as the American Robin, vary only slightly, with the female being a lighter color. The males of one species in particular, the House Finch, have great variety in their coloration. They can range in color from wine red to gold-yellow. This difference is, supposedly, dependent upon diet.

All birds go through at least one molt a year, after breeding season. In some urban yard species, especially the warblers, the males (sometimes the females) may assume a breeding coloration different from that of the nonbreeding season, usually during a pre-breeding-season molt. So, this means that you can see different colored feathers on the same birds at different times of year!

Every species can produce albinos: birds with white feathers instead of the usual colors of their species. There can be total albinism (rare) or partial, which may involve only some of the feathers. Partial is the most common form.

Another twist is the young bird. Most birds, upon leaving the nest (called "fledging") resemble but do not completely look like the adult of their species. For example, the young Scrub Jay has not developed its full blue color, and it will not do so until its second year. Some fledglings look altogether different in color. A good example of this is the Robin; the young retain their spots through the first winter.

To make matters worse, the actual color you see on the bird's feathers may depend on the lighting. In dull light, you may not even see the most brilliant of colors well.

In addition to differing colors in feathers, birds often have more subtle differences in the colors of their bills, legs, and feet. This will become more important as you begin learning to tell very similar species apart.

Three: Young vs. Nestling vs. Fledgling vs. Juvenile vs. Immature.
I guess this is as good a time as any to discuss terms that apply to the young of a species. All pre-adult birds can be referred to as "young." The term "nestling" refers to the time from hatching until the young bird leaves the nest. The bird is then referred to as a "fledgling." "Juvenile" refers to a young bird that has fledged and is able to care for itself but has not completed its molt from nestling plumage. "Immature," in general, refers to a young bird during its first year of life, before it has acquired adult plumage. Some species may remain as immatures for several years (in this case, they are referred to as "subadults"). Confusing, huh?

Four: Resident vs. Visitor vs. Migrant.
Some bird species occur in southern California year-round and are referred to as "resident" birds. They may shift their home areas slightly during the year to take advantage of the food and weather changes, but basically you can observe them in the same general area at any time of year. Examples of such birds would be the California Towhee, Spotted Towhee, Scrub Jay, and Mockingbird.

Other birds, called "visitors," occur in southern California at specific times of year, and normally, you would not be able to find them at other times. There are two types of visitors:

Those that occur during the *breeding season,* when they are here to breed and then return "home" to more tropical areas in Central or South America. Examples of breeding-season visitors are Hooded Orioles and Black-headed Grosbeaks.

Those that occur during the *winter season* to take advantage of the milder climate and more abundant food. They continue northward to their breeding grounds when the conditions are right. Examples of winter visitors are Yellow-rumped Warblers and Cedar Waxwings.

"Migrants" are those species that only stop in the Inland Empire briefly to refuel before continuing on their journey to or from their breeding grounds. Stopover migrants include Warbling Vireos and Black-throated Gray Warblers.

Five: Territoriality. The size of a bird's territory depends upon the species and the time of year. Most birds only defend their territories during the breeding season, when the male and female are protecting their nest site. After breeding season is finished, many species of birds will band together in what is called a "mixed-species flock" and just roam around an area searching for food. In the winter, some species, such as the Mockingbird, remain in pairs and defend a smaller territory. Other species, including the Robin, will flock together.

The House Finch and others have very small territories and are considered "semicolonial." In other words, they share very close quarters when nesting. Other species, such as Acorn Woodpeckers, are "cooperative breeders" that live in family groups. The young, fledged from previous years, help raise their siblings.

Six: Feeding Habits. Birds can be divided into categories based on their feeding preferences: what they eat and where and how they feed. Some, such as the Mockingbird and House Sparrow, are habitat generalists; they will eat just about anything available. The generalists do well in cities and suburbs because of the large variety of foods that humans provide, directly or indirectly. We grow a vast array of ornamental plants in our yards, and we provide handouts in the way of feeders. We inadvertently feed birds from weeds and garbage. Habitat specialists, such as the Phainopepla, often cannot live entirely within the confines of a city or suburb. They require food from specific sources that humans usually do not provide.

Most bird species, even those that predominantly eat seeds or drink nectar, provide insects to their young. Insects have a much higher protein content and other nutrients that the young need to grow. Therefore, the use of pesticides during breeding season could be detrimental to bird populations and the raising of young.

If you look at various bird species closely, you will notice different shaped bills. The shape actually corresponds to the type of food normally eaten by that species. For example, seedeaters, such as the House Finch, tend to have broad, thick bills that are powerful enough to crack open seeds. Jays and Crows have such strong bills that they can actually hammer seeds open. Birds that catch flying insects, such as the Black Phoebe, have flat, broad bills that allow them to pick their prey from the air with ease. Insect eaters that search through plants for food usually have thinner, sharper bills that can glean insects off leaves. Birds that feed primarily on nectar will have bills shaped to fit into the flowers of the plants they usually feed upon. Hummingbirds often feed on long, tubular flowers and, therefore, have long bills.

Birds often will change food sources, depending upon availability. An example of this is the Robin, which eats mostly insects and worms but will switch to fruit when it is available.

Seven: The Best Viewing Season. Breeding season is the optimum time for us to observe birds and their behaviors. In southern California, this can begin as early as January and continue through August, depending upon weather conditions. But most nesting activity takes place between mid-March and June. After this, things quiet down a lot in the bird world, as birds often travel outside their breeding territories in mixed-species flocks. Other birds are getting ready to migrate south and may be wandering in search of the best food resources to help them prepare for the journey.

Fall is a good time to look for migrants, those birds just passing through on their way farther south. Winter affords us a view of birds we don't see during breeding season, such as Yellow-rumped Warblers and Cedar Waxwings.

Eight: The Best Viewing Times. You can see more birds in the morning and early evening. During the breeding season, have you noticed the din in the morning, when all the birds seem to be calling and singing at once? This is called the "dawn chorus," when birds are resuming their activities, such as nest building and feeding, after their night's rest. Birds are referred to as "crepuscular," meaning that they are most active at both ends of the day. During the hotter parts of the day, they engage in roosting, preening, sleeping, and other less active pastimes.

Nine: How to Figure Out "Which Bird That Is." Over time, you will get better at this. Honest. Unfortunately, birds don't give you much time to see them (they're usually there and gone). The best thing to do is observe everything you can, *quickly!* If you have a partner in this effort, one of you can look at the book while the other describes the bird, without taking his or her eyes off it. And remember, having a pair of binoculars really helps! Look for:

- The *color, shape,* and *size* of the bird (compare it to a bird you know, like a sparrow or robin)
- The *shape of the bill* (is it thin, fat, short, long?)
- The *shape of the tail* (long, short, round, notched?)
- Any noticeable *behaviors* (for example, does it flick its tail?)

Then, look at this book. Refer to the lists and apply what you know of the bird's size, behavior, color, and so on.

Eventually, you will be able to recognize birds by groups (often families). This allows you to categorize more quickly and greatly reduce your choices when trying to identify a new bird. For example, if you can place a bird in the finch or wren group, you will eliminate a vast number of choices and be able to check a field guide for one specific group.

There will be birds that look very similar, such as a male Spotted Towhee and a male Black-headed Grosbeak. Knowing the *behaviors* of both species will help you identify them. For example, the towhee spends its time scratching around in litter under shrubs. The grosbeak, on the other hand, feeds primarily in shrubs and trees.

Know *when* to expect to see a specific bird, to help narrow down your choices. If it's wintertime, you know you won't see a Black-headed Grosbeak, since it doesn't show up in our area until spring. If it's summer, you won't see a White-crowned Sparrow.

Sound overwhelming? I suggest learning to identify the more brightly colored males first, since they are usually more easily identifiable and are less confusing. Then add the females and immatures. In spite of it all, there will still be those birds that always confound you. This even happens to advanced birders. I have created some "look-alike" pages for you to refer to. They will help you learn the most similar-looking species and their differences. *Good luck!*

Ten: Parts of a Bird. It is important to know the terms for the basic parts of a bird. Please refer to a field guide if you need more detail.

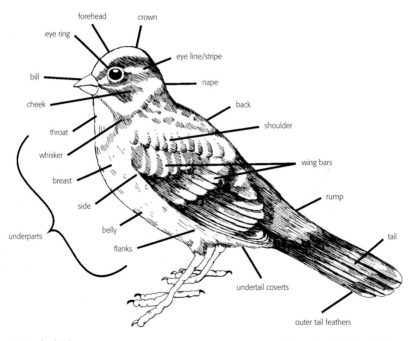

Parts of a bird

Illustration by Melissa Badalian

LISTS OF COMMON
INLAND EMPIRE YARD BIRDS

MOST LIKELY TO BE SEEN

Yard Birds: Permanent, Year-Round Residents and Breeders

Most Common

(Those you could most likely see often and regularly in your yard)

Anna's Hummingbird

American Crow

European Starling

House Finch

House Sparrow

Northern Mockingbird

Less Common

Acorn Woodpecker

Band-tailed Pigeon

Cooper's Hawk

Nuttall's Woodpecker

Red-shouldered Hawk

Spotted Towhee

Nighttime Birds

Barn Owl

Great Horned Owl

Western Screech Owl

Next Most Common Residents

(Those you may see less often, but regularly, in your yard)

American Robin

Bewick's Wren

Black Phoebe

Brown-headed Cowbird

Bushtit

California Towhee

House Wren

Lesser Goldfinch

Mourning Dove

Rock Dove (Pigeon)

Song Sparrow

Western Scrub Jay

Predominantly "Edge Species"

(Usually only seen if your yard backs up to open space, such as Box Springs Mountain, Sycamore Canyon, Mount Rubidoux, or the Santa Ana River)

American Kestrel

Brewer's Blackbird

Costa's Hummingbird

Greater Roadrunner

Killdeer

Phainopepla

Red-tailed Hawk

VISITORS

Breeding Visitors Only

Black-chinned Hummingbird

Cliff Swallow

Hooded Oriole

Winter Visitors Only

American Goldfinch (except along the Santa Ana River, where it is year-round)

Cedar Waxwing

Chipping Sparrow (also a migrant)

Dark-eyed Junco

Northern Flicker (a few individuals are permanent)

Orange-crowned Warbler

Pine Siskin

Ruby-crowned Kinglet

Western Bluebird*

White-crowned Sparrow

Yellow-rumped Warbler

Migrating through in Spring or Fall

(This is only a list of the most commonly seen)

Black-headed Grosbeak (some do breed in less urbanized areas)

Black-throated Gray Warbler

Bullock's Oriole

Hermit Thrush

Swallow species (Barn Swallow, Violet-green Swallow, Rough-winged Swallow, and Tree Swallow) form large migrating groups

Warbling Vireo

Wilson's Warbler

Western Tanager

Other birds that you might see, but much less often, are listed in *Unusual Birds You Might See in Your Yard.*

---

*Due to urbanization and loss of nesting sites in trees, the Riverside-Corona Resource Conservation District works to provide nest boxes through the spring. Volunteers place and monitor them, helping to increase Western Bluebird and other native bird populations in the Inland Empire.

BIRDS BY SIZE

The size (total length) of a bird is measured from the tip of the bill to the tip of the tail. I often use the American Robin and the House Sparrow as reference points when referring to general sizes of birds. They are in bold type here for ease of reference.

Large: 14 to 23 inches

Greater Roadrunner	23"
Great Horned Owl	22"
Red-tailed Hawk	22"
Red-shouldered Hawk	19"
American Crow	17½"
Barn Owl	16"
Cooper's Hawk	14–20"
Band-tailed Pigeon	14½"

Medium-large: 10 to 13 inches

Northern Flicker	12½"
Rock Dove Pigeon	12½"
Mourning Dove	12"
Western Scrub Jay	11½"
American Kestrel	10½"
Killdeer	10½"
American Robin	**10"**
Northern Mockingbird	10"

Medium: 6½ to 9 inches

Acorn Woodpecker	9"
Brewer's Blackbird	9"
Western Screech Owl	9"
Bullock's Oriole	8¾"
California Towhee	8½"
European Starling	8½"
Spotted Towhee	8½"
Black-headed Grosbeak	8¼"
Hooded Oriole	8"
Phainopepla	7¾"
Brown-headed Cowbird	7½"
Nuttall's Woodpecker	7½"
Cedar Waxwing	7¼"
Western Tanager	7¼"
Western Bluebird	7"
White-crowned Sparrow	7"
Black Phoebe	6¾"
Hermit Thrush	6¾"

Small: 5 to 6¼ inches

Dark-eyed Junco	6¼"
House Sparrow	6¼"
Song Sparrow	6¼"
House Finch	6"
Cliff Swallow	5½"
Warbling Vireo	5½"
Yellow-rumped Warbler	5½"
Bewick's Wren	5¼"
American Goldfinch	5"
Black-throated Gray Warbler	5"
Orange-crowned Warbler	5"
Pine Siskin	5"

Very Small: 3½ to 4¾ inches

House Wren	4¾"
Wilson's Warbler	4¾"
Bushtit	4½"
Lesser Goldfinch	4½"
Ruby-crowned Kinglet	4¼"
Anna's Hummingbird	4"
Black-chinned Hummingbird	3¾"
Costa's Hummingbird	3½"

BIRDS BY BEHAVIOR

Feed Primarily on, or Close to, the Ground

American Crow

Brewer's Blackbird

Brown-headed Cowbird

California Towhee

Dark-eyed Junco

European Starling

Greater Roadrunner

House Finch

House Sparrow

Killdeer

Mourning Dove

Northern Flicker

Rock Dove (Pigeon)

Spotted Towhee

White-crowned Sparrow

Perch on Branches, Telephone Poles and Wires, and Other High Places while Searching for Food

American Kestrel

Black Phoebe

Cooper's Hawk

Great Horned Owl

Red-shouldered Hawk

Red-tailed Hawk

Western Bluebird

Western Screech Owl

Western Scrub Jay

Feed Primarily in Shrubs and Trees

Acorn Woodpecker

American Goldfinch

American Robin

Anna's Hummingbird

Band-tailed Pigeon

Bewick's Wren

Black-chinned Hummingbird

Black-headed Grosbeak

Black-throated Gray Warbler

Bullock's Oriole

Bushtit

Cedar Waxwing

Costa's Hummingbird

Hermit Thrush

Hooded Oriole

House Wren

Lesser Goldfinch

Northern Mockingbird

Nuttall's Woodpecker

Orange-crowned Warbler

Phainopepla

Pine Siskin

Ruby-crowned Kinglet

Song Sparrow

Warbling Vireo

Western Tanager

Wilson's Warbler

Yellow-rumped Warbler

Feed on the Wing

Barn Owl

Cliff Swallow

Usually Seen in Groups

Acorn Woodpecker

American Crow

American Goldfinch

American Robin

Band-tailed Pigeon

Barn Swallow

Brewer's Blackbird

Brown-headed Cowbird

Bushtit

Cedar Waxwing

Cliff Swallow

Dark-eyed Junco

European Starling

House Finch

House Sparrow

Lesser Goldfinch

Mourning Dove

Pine Siskin

Rock Dove

Western Bluebird

White-crowned Sparrow

Usually Seen Alone or with a Mate

American Kestrel

Anna's Hummingbird

Barn Owl

Bewick's Wren

Black Phoebe

Black-chinned Hummingbird

Black-headed Grosbeak

Black-throated Gray Warbler

Bullock's Oriole

California Towhee

Cooper's Hawk

Costa's Hummingbird

Great Horned Owl

Greater Roadrunner

Hermit Thrush

Hooded Oriole

House Wren

Northern Flicker

Northern Mockingbird

Nuttall's Woodpecker

Orange-crowned Warbler

Phainopepla

Red-shouldered Hawk

Red-tailed Hawk

Ruby-crowned Kinglet

Song Sparrow

Spotted Towhee

Warbling Vireo

Western Screech Owl

Western Scrub Jay

Western Tanager

Wilson's Warbler

Yellow-rumped Warbler

Open-cup Nesters

American Crow

American Goldfinch

American Robin

Anna's Hummingbird

Band-tailed Pigeon

Barn Swallow

Black Phoebe

Black-chinned Hummingbird

Black-headed Grosbeak

Black-throated Gray Warbler

Brewer's Blackbird

Brown-headed Cowbird

Bullock's Oriole

Bushtit

California Towhee

Cedar Waxwing

Cliff Swallow

Cooper's Hawk

Costa's Hummingbird

Dark-eyed Junco

Great Horned Owl

Greater Roadrunner

Hermit Thrush

Hooded Oriole

House Finch

House Sparrow

Killdeer

Lesser Goldfinch

Mourning Dove

Northern Mockingbird

Orange-crowned Warbler

Phainopepla

Pine Siskin

Red-shouldered Hawk

Red-tailed Hawk

Rock Dove

Ruby-crowned Kinglet

Song Sparrow

Spotted Towhee

Warbling Vireo

Western Scrub Jay

Western Tanager

White-crowned Sparrow

Wilson's Warbler

Yellow-rumped Warbler

Cavity Nesters

Acorn Woodpecker

American Kestrel

Barn Owl

Bewick's Wren

European Starling

House Wren

Northern Flicker

Western Bluebird

Western Screech Owl

Flicker cavity, Bear Paw Ranch   Photo by Sheila Kee

BIRDS BY GROUP

Groups of birds share outward characteristics, such as silhouette, shape of bill or tail, body size, and behavior. Because field guides are organized taxonomically, it helps tremendously to learn birds by these group characteristics (usually by family); if you can place a bird in a group, you will be better able to locate its description in a field guide.

Bushtits

Tiny birds; long tails; large, twittering flocks; hanging nests.

Bushtit

Crows and Jays

Large birds; heavy bills; intelligent, aggressive, gregarious; raucous voices.

American Crow

Common Raven

Western Scrub Jay

Cuckoos

Long, slender tails; two toes forward, two toes back.

Greater Roadrunner

Falcons

Long, narrow, pointed wings; females larger than males.

American Kestrel

Finches

Small seedeaters; undulating flight; usually in flocks.

American Goldfinch

House Finch

Lesser Goldfinch

Pine Siskin

Flycatchers

Large heads; erect posture; broad, flat bills snap when catching insects.

Black Phoebe

Hawks

Large birds; hooked bills; large feet with strong claws; rounded wings; long tails; females larger than males; diurnal

Cooper's Hawk

Red-shouldered Hawk

Red-tailed Hawk

Hummingbirds

Long, needlelike bills and grooved tongues allow them to feed on flower nectar; rapid wingbeat, hovering flight, can fly backwards.

Anna's Hummingbird

Black-chinned Hummingbird

Costa's Hummingbird

Old World Sparrows

Short legs; thick bills.

House Sparrow

Orioles and Blackbirds

Sharp, pointed bills; strong, direct flight.

Brewer's Blackbird

Brown-headed Cowbird

Bullock's Oriole

Hooded Oriole

Owls

Large heads; short necks; two toes forward, two backward; large eyes are fixed in their sockets, so they must move the entire head to look at something; primarily nocturnal; regurgitate pellets.

Barn Owl

Great Horned Owl

Western Screech Owl

Pigeons and Doves

Plump bodies; small, bobbing heads; strong, fast flyers.

Band-tailed Pigeon

Mourning Dove

Rock Dove (Pigeon)

Plovers

Compact bodies; long legs; bills swell at tip; pointed wings; birds dart across ground with sudden stops; flight is direct and fast.

Killdeer

Silky Flycatchers

Slender; crested heads; soft, sleek plumage.

Phainopepla

Sparrows and Warblers

Related genetically, although outwardly different.

Black-headed Grosbeak

California Towhee

Dark-eyed Junco

Orange-crowned Warbler

Song Sparrow

Spotted Towhee

White-crowned Sparrow

Wilson's Warbler

Yellow-rumped Warbler

Starlings

Chunky, dark, glossy bodies; gregarious.

European Starling

Swallows

Slender bodies; small legs and feet; long, pointed wings; swift, adept, darting flight.

Cliff Swallow

Thrushes and Mimic Thrushes

Narrow bills; often eloquent singers.

American Robin

Hermit Thrush

Northern Mockingbird

Ruby-crowned Kinglet

Western Bluebird

Waxwings

Sleek, crested heads; silky plumage; yellow-tipped tails; red, waxy tips at ends of feathers.

Cedar Waxwing

Wrens

Small, chunky bodies; slender, curved bills; up-tilted tails; loud and territorial; move constantly in search of food.

Bewick's Wren

House Wren

Woodpeckers

Short legs; stiff tails; sharply pointed bills; strong claws; two toes forward, two backward.

Acorn Woodpecker

Northern Flicker

Nuttall's Woodpecker

SPECIES DESCRIPTIONS

Arranged by Conspicuous Color

BLUE ACCENTS

Western Bluebird

Sialia mexicana

Spanish name: Azulejo gorjiazul

When can I expect to see them? Western Bluebirds are primarily winter visitors, occurring between November and April. They are fairly common in the Inland Empire during this time, although numbers seem to vary from year to year. Some pairs do remain in the summer and nest.

What do they look like? The Western Bluebird is slightly larger than a House Sparrow, being about 7 inches long. The males maintain their vibrant blue plumage all year. Their heads, throats, wings, and tails are a deep purple-blue. The breast is chestnut (rust-colored), as is the upper back on most males. The female is a brownish gray overall, with the tail and wings being a light shade of blue. She has a gray throat and chestnut breast.

The juveniles have spotted breasts; bluebirds are related to the robins and thrushes. You probably will not see many juveniles, since Western Bluebirds infrequently nest in the Inland Empire.

Similar species: Other than the Western Scrub Jay, the Western Bluebird is the only blue-colored bird that you would probably see on a regular basis in your yard. The Mountain Bluebird (not discussed), also a winter visitor, is seen much less frequently. Steller's Jays (not discussed) may also be here on an irregular basis.

Western Bluebird female

Western Bluebird male

Although the American Robin also has red underparts, its back is dark gray, rather than the deep blue of the Bluebird.

Behaviors: Western Bluebirds occur in flocks during the winter and are seen in mixed-species flocks with Cedar Waxwings, Yellow-rumped Warblers, and Robins.

Voice: The best way to describe the Western Bluebird's call is that it sounds like someone plucking on a large rubber band; they often give this call as they fly. The male has no real song, even during breeding season.

Nesting: Western Bluebirds do not nest in the Inland Empire in large numbers. Although some pairs do nest along the Santa Ana River, most travel farther north and into the nearby mountains, to nest near the meadows.

Food: Western Bluebirds are primarily insect eaters. They perch in low branches of trees and then fly down to the ground to catch beetles, caterpillars, crickets, snails, and spiders. They will also eat berries and fruit in the winter.

Will they use my yard? Bluebirds can be seen in suburban yards that provide fruit and berries in the winter. They also are attracted to mealworms placed on platform feeders. I have attracted them into my yard by providing water for bathing and drinking.

Being cavity nesters, Bluebirds may use nest boxes placed high in tree branches, adjacent to large grassy areas; the grass is home to the insects that they eat. The entrance hole size should be no larger than one and a half inches, to prevent Starlings from entering and taking over.

In the eastern United States and along the California coast, Bluebird populations were in serious decline until people started providing boxes for nesting. Volunteers from the Riverside-Corona Resource Conservation District place nest boxes in parks and along golf courses to attract Bluebirds to breed in the greater Riverside area. Historically, Bluebirds nested inland, but with urbanization there are fewer tree cavities to nest in. Also, introduced and more aggressive species, such as Starlings, have taken over many of the few remaining nest sites.

Key things to look for:
1) Sparrow-sized. **2)** Blue backs, tails, and wings. **3)** Rusty underparts.

Western Scrub Jay   *Aphelocoma californica*

Spanish name: Chara azuleja

In most bird books, the Western Scrub Jay is still referred to as the Scrub Jay. Adding to the confusion, people often refer to them as "blue jays," although the actual Blue Jay has a crest and only occurs in the Midwest and east of the Mississippi.

When can I expect to see them? Western Scrub Jays are resident birds and breeders of the Inland Empire, native to the western United States. They are the most widespread of the western jays and have been able to expand their range due to human settlement.

What do they look like? The Western Scrub Jay is slightly larger than a Robin, and both sexes look alike. The head, wings, and long tail are blue. The back is pale, bluish gray. The head is crestless and the throat is white, bordered by a blue-gray "necklace" below it.

Immatures are overall grayer than adults and have more distinct streaking on their chests. They maintain this plumage until early fall, at which point they take on the look of an adult.

Similar species: The Inland Empire's only other blue-colored bird is the Western Bluebird, which is smaller and a much more brilliant blue.

Western Scrub Jay

The Northern Mockingbird is of similar size and shape, but gray overall with white wing patches.

Behaviors: Scrub Jays are intelligent birds, as are all members of the crow family. They can be seen sitting on telephone wires and on the tops of trees, with their long tails drooping downward. They bob up and down as a defensive posture. They can be seen hopping along the ground in search of food, moving both feet simultaneously. They have an undulating flight pattern and often call as they fly.

Voice: Scrub Jays have a loud, emphatic, raucous call, which sounds like one or a series of shrieks. These calls act as warning alarms for other birds. Scrub Jays have no real song.

Nesting: Scrub Jays build stick nests in dense shrubbery or small trees. They are very secretive and quiet while nesting. They stay paired with their mate all year and have a permanent, year-round territory. They may have "helpers" at the nest, which are the young of the previous year.

The female lays four to six bluish green eggs with darker markings over the entire surface. The young are born altricial. The male does some of the incubating, which lasts about two weeks.

Food: During breeding season, Scrub Jays tend to eat insects (grasshoppers, wasps, bees, beetles, caterpillars, flies) and spiders. They will also eat smaller birds, especially eggs and nestlings, and this includes poultry young and eggs. During nonbreeding season, Scrub Jays eat more plant materials: fruit, acorns, pine seeds, sunflower seeds, nuts, and berries. They will also store nuts and seeds for later use in various places, even under a few leaves on the ground. They are capable of remembering where they stored the food, even months later.

Will they use my yard? Grow sunflowers, and they will come! Scrub Jays will readily visit feeder tables, especially if offered sunflower seeds. But because of their size and aggressiveness, they may scare away smaller birds. They also may decimate your supply of bird food in no time, due to their fondness for storing seed. They are also attracted to suet and fresh water.

Key things to look for:
1) Robin-sized. **2)** Blue and gray. **3)** Undulating flight. **4)** Loud call.

YELLOW ACCENTS

Lesser Goldfinch

Carduelis psaltria

Spanish name: Dominico dorsioscuro

The Lesser Goldfinch used to be called the Green-backed Goldfinch.

When can I expect to see them? The Lesser Goldfinches are year-round residents and breeders of the Inland Empire, so expect them in your yard at any time.

What do they look like? Lesser Goldfinches are small birds, a mere 4½ inches long. In southern California we have the green-backed form, where the male is dark greenish above and bright yellow below, with a black cap, wings, and tail. The female is greenish above, with no black cap, and a duller yellow below. Both the male and female have patches of pure white in the middle of each wing that can be seen when they fly. They have short, conical bills.

Similar species: The female Lesser Goldfinch could be easily confused with the female American Goldfinch and possibly with the female Yellow-rumped Warbler. The best way to distinguish the female Lesser and American Goldfinches is to look for the white undertail coverts. If the bird has them, it's an American. If there is no white under the tail, it's a Lesser Goldfinch. The female Yellow-rumped Warbler does not have

Lesser Goldfinch female *Lesser Goldfinch male*

the white wing patches and has a yellow rump and some yellow on the head and under the throat.

Behaviors: Lesser Goldfinches, like all Goldfinch species, have an undulating flight. They are highly gregarious during most of the year, except when nesting. They may be difficult to see, since they are small and active and scattered among the tree leaves. So learn to listen for their calls.

Voice: The Lesser Goldfinch has a plaintive, mournful sigh that acts as its call. It is a descending slurred note which sounds like "tee-yee." The male has a song that is long and consists of variable musical notes. The male gives its call notes and song as it flies or when it is perched.

Nesting: In your yard, the Lesser Goldfinch will build its cup nest in shrubs or trees, anywhere from two to thirty feet above the ground. The Goldfinch especially likes to be near water. The nest will be well concealed by leaves and twigs. The female builds the nest (with some help from the male) of plant fibers and grass stems. She lines it with down, a few feathers, and other soft materials. She lays four to five pale blue, unmarked eggs and incubates them for about two weeks. The male feeds her while she incubates. The Lesser Goldfinch usually will have two broods per year.

Food: Lesser Goldfinches are strictly seedeaters. They will eat seeds from weeds, grasses, and trees, such as the western sycamore, alder, and birch. The Goldfinches do not like to feed on the ground but will hang on to the sides of dried plants, seed heads, or grasses for support as they feed. In the winter particularly, they will appear in mixed-species flocks to feed.

Will they use my yard? Lesser Goldfinches most often can be seen in yards that have drier, "weedier" areas, or in yards that have trees that produce the catkins that they like to eat, such as alder and birch. They *love* thistle seeds, which have a high fat content, and will flock to hanging tube feeders that provide thistle! They will also eat small sunflower seeds and millet provided at feeders.

Key things to look for:
1) Small greenish and black bird. **2)** Yellow underparts. **3)** No white undertail coverts. **4)** Distinctive white patches on the wings when flying.

Wilson's Warbler

Wilsonia pusilla

Spanish name: Chipe de Wilson

When can I expect to see them? Wilson's Warblers are fairly common spring and fall migrants through the Inland Empire. The peak of spring migration is April, and the peak of fall migration is September.

What do they look like? Wilson's Warblers are small, slender birds that are olive-green above and bright yellow underneath, with an all-dark tail. The male has a yellow face and a small, noticeable, black cap. The females and immatures have more olive-colored caps and yellowish foreheads.

Similar species: The Wilson's Warbler could be confused with an American Goldfinch in breeding plumage, since they are both yellow and black and of similar size. However, the Wilson's Warbler has an all-dark tail, whereas the American Goldfinch has white on both the upper tail and undertail coverts. The wings of the Wilson's Warbler do not have the white wing bars or shoulder patches of the Goldfinch. Behaviorally, Goldfinches tend to be seen in flocks, whereas the Warblers are more solitary.

Wilson's Warbler female

Behaviors: Wilson's Warblers are fairly active birds, moving through shrubs and the lower branches of trees in search of insects. So in spite of their bright color, they are not often easy to see.

Voice: The male has an abrupt, hurried "chee-chee-chee" song that goes slightly down in pitch at the end. The call is a sharp "chip."

Nesting: The Wilson's Warbler does not commonly nest in suburban areas, but chooses more riparian areas, along streams with dense thickets.

Food: The Wilson's Warbler is an insect eater that usually stays within ten feet of the ground when feeding. It jerks its tail as it gleans insects from leaves. It will also dart into the air after insects. In the fall, Wilson's Warblers eat some fruit in addition to insects.

Will they use my yard? Wilson's Warblers are known to use suburban yards that have shrubs and provide undergrowth, since they like to stay fairly close to the ground. During migration, Wilson's Warblers would most likely be attracted to a yard that provides a birdbath or other water source.

Key things to look for:
1) Small, yellow bird. **2)** All-dark tail. **3)** Black cap (male) or olive-colored cap (female).

Wilson's Warbler male

American Goldfinch

Carduelis tristis

Spanish name: Dominico Americano

Often called a Wild Canary.

When can I expect to see them? You're most likely to see American Goldfinches in the fall and winter, when the numbers of birds swell in the Inland Empire. They are, however, permanent residents along the Santa Ana River, so they can be seen all year if you live nearby.

American Goldfinch female

What do they look like? The American Goldfinch is one of the few birds we have in the Inland Empire that can be seen in winter plumage, when both adults and immatures are gray or brown above and pale yellow below. The male may show some of the black cap and yellow shoulder patch of his breeding plumage.

If you are lucky enough to see the male in breeding plumage, you

American Goldfinch male
in breeding plumage

American Goldfinch male
in nonbreeding plumage

will be amazed at the difference. He has a bright yellow head and body and a black cap, wings, and tail.

The American Goldfinch, no matter what age, sex, or plumage, has white wing bars and a white rump and undertail coverts.

Similar species: The best way to distinguish the American Goldfinch from the Lesser Goldfinch (male, female, or immature, in any plumage), is to note the white on the American's rump and under the tail. The male could also be confused with a Wilson's Warbler, although the Wilson's does not have any white on it.

Behaviors: American Goldfinches are gregarious and are often seen in mixed-species flocks in the winter, especially with Lesser Goldfinches and Pine Siskins. They have an undulating flight like the Lesser Goldfinches.

Voice: The male's song is a lively series of trills, twitters, and "swee" notes. Both sexes also have a distinctive flight call that sounds like "per-chik-o-ree."

Nesting: Beginning in April, the female selects a nest site, which is usually in a shrub or tree, and builds a cup nest of woven plant fibers lined with plant down. She lays four to six very pale blue, unmarked eggs and incubates them for about two weeks. The male and female tend the young, which are born altricial but are able to leave the nest in about two weeks. The nestlings are fed entirely on seeds that the adults partly digest and then regurgitate.

Food: American Goldfinches eat mainly seeds, of birch, alder, and conifers especially, as well as seeds of many annual plants. They will also eat some insects and fruit.

Will they use my yard? The winter flocks can be seen in many residential areas, feeding on lawns and weedy fields as well as on catkins of trees like alder and sycamore. American Goldfinches love sunflower and thistle seeds. If you offer the seeds in a hanging feeder, they will probably show up in your yard in the winter if they are in the area. If they have trouble at first locating your feeder, tie a yellow ribbon around the top of the tube. They may think the ribbon is another finch and come to investigate.

Key things to look for:
1) Small. **2)** Bright or pale yellow, varies with time of year. **3)** White on the rump and under the tail. **4)** In a flock. **5)** Undulating flight.

Pine Siskin

Carduelis pinus

Spanish name: Dominico pinero

When can I expect to see them? Pine Siskins are considered erratic visitors to the Inland Empire area. They may appear in fairly large numbers one year and virtually disappear the next. So keep your eyes (and ears) open!

What do they look like? The Pine Siskin is small with prominent brown streaking and yellow flight feathers, which are noticeable in flight. It also has yellow at the base of the tail. The bill of the Siskin is thin. The male and female look alike.

Similar species: The Pine Siskin could be confused with streaked female Sparrows and female House Finches, which do not have the yellow coloring, are larger, and have thicker bills (see **Look-alikes**). A male House Finch that has yellow plumage, rather than the normal red, could also be confused with a Pine Siskin.

Behaviors: In winter, Pine Siskins occur in mixed flocks with other finches. Siskins have undulating flight like other finches.

Pine Siskin adult

Voice: The call of the Pine Siskin sounds like a high-pitched zipper closing. It is a "zzzzzzttttt" sound that rises in pitch, especially at the end.

Nesting: Pine Siskins nest in coniferous and mixed forests of the mountains.

Food: In the winter, when they are in the Inland Empire, the Pine Siskins will frequent seed-bearing trees, such as conifers, alder, sycamore, and birch.

Will they use my yard? Pine Siskins may be attracted naturally to your area if you have conifers and seed-bearing trees. They will feed at bird feeders if provided thistle and cracked sunflower seeds. They are also attracted to water.

Key things to look for:
1) Small. **2)** Heavily streaked. **3)** Yellow in wings and at base of tail.
4) Undulating flight. **5)** In a flock.

Orange-Crowned Warbler

Vermivora celata

Spanish name: Chipe corona-naranja

When can I expect to see them? Some Orange-crowned Warblers are winter visitors in the Inland Empire, arriving in September. Others migrate through during spring and fall.

What do they look like? The Orange-crowned Warbler is one of the most nondescript birds in our area, with no wing bars or other distinguishable markings. In this respect, it is quite distinctive! The ages and sexes look similar, with their olive-green heads and upperparts, and greenish yellow underparts, slightly streaked on the sides. Both sexes have an orange crown, but it is rarely seen.

Similar species: The Orange-crowned Warbler could be confused with any other nondescript bird, such as the female sparrow. The thing to remember is to look at the bill shape; the warblers have thin bills for insect-eating, and the sparrows have more stout, seed-eating bills. The Ruby-crowned Kinglet, which is also a winter visitor, is smaller and has white wing bars but no yellowish wash and no streaking at all.

Behaviors: Orange-crowned Warblers are lively and flit around the tips of branches. They are sometimes seen in loose flocks with other warblers.

Orange-crowned Warbler female
Orange-crowned Warbler male

Voice: Orange-crowned Warblers have a light, rapid "chit-chit-chit" call that slides downwards.

Nesting: Orange-crowned Warblers do not nest in the more urban or suburban areas, but in dense thickets of riparian trees in the mountains or in chaparral on steep slopes. They arrive at their breeding grounds in early April.

Food: Orange-crowned Warblers primarily eat insects and are especially fond of flowering eucalyptus, where a lot of insects can be found. They also eat some berries.

Will they use my yard? Orange-crowned Warblers are fairly common in suburban yards, although they are so nondescript that they often go unnoticed. They will eat at feeding stations that provide them suet, peanut butter, and even doughnuts (although these are as lacking in nutrients for them as for us)!

Key things to look for:
1) Small. **2)** Nondescript. **3)** Olive-green above. **4)** No wing bars.
5) Yellowish wash underneath. **6)** Thin bill.

Variation in color of Orange-crowned Warbler

Yellow-Rumped Warbler

Dendroica coronata

Spanish name: Chipe rabadilla-amarilla

The western populations of Yellow-rumped Warblers are also known as Audubon's Warblers. Until recently they were considered a separate species from the eastern population of Yellow-rumped Warblers, which some people still refer to as Myrtle Warblers.

When can I expect to see them? Yellow-rumped Warblers are winter visitors to the Inland Empire, showing up in early October and leaving by mid-May.

What do they look like? Yellow-rumped Warblers are small birds (5¼ inches) with slender bills. They have yellow rumps, yellow crown patches, and yellow patches on their sides and throats. Their dark tails have white spots on the outside corners. The males have a breeding and nonbreeding plumage. The nonbreeding (winter) plumage is a lighter shade of yellow, similar to the females' year-round plumage. Yellow-rumped Warblers vary greatly in color by age and sex.

Similar species: Fortunately (from an identification perspective only), the other gray-and-yellow warblers that the Yellow-rumped could be confused with don't occur regularly in the Inland Empire.

Yellow-rumped Warbler male in breeding plumage

Behaviors: Yellow-rumped Warblers are gregarious and may be seen in loose flocks. During the winter the male and female do not stay paired. The Yellow-rumped Warbler is an active bird that is continually moving in search of prey.

Voice: The males have slow, warbling songs, but you normally won't hear them sing while they are visitors in the Inland Empire. You will, however, frequently hear the soft "chit" call made by both the male and female.

Nesting: Yellow-rumped Warblers do not nest in the Inland Empire; they nest in the conifer forests of the western mountains.

Food: Yellow-rumped Warblers are predominantly insect eaters. They feed on the ground by flycatching, and by catching insects while flitting through the tree branches. In the fall and winter they will also eat small amounts of fruits and berries.

Will they use my yard? Yellow-rumped Warblers will, potentially, use any suburban yard that has insects. I have attracted Yellow-rumped Warblers by providing water for drinking and bathing.

Key things to look for:
1) Fairly small, thin, gray-and-yellow bird. **2)** Yellow rump.
3) Pale yellow on the crown, throat, and sides. **4)** Thin bill.

Yellow-rumped Warbler female

RED ACCENTS

House Finch

Carpodacus mexicanus

Spanish name: Fringilido Mexicano

House Finch female (above), male (below)

Some people refer to the House Finch as a Linnet.

When can I expect to see them? House Finches are abundant in the Inland Empire all year, as they are permanent residents and breeders. They are native to the western states but in the 1940s they were introduced, illegally, to the East Coast by pet breeders and were called "Hollywood Finches." Since then, they have become common in much of the East, and their range is still expanding.

What do they look like? The House Finch is small, only 6 inches long. The most distinctive thing about the males is their red color. However, the male House Finch can be highly variable in color, from yellow to orange to deep red on his forehead, throat, and rump. He is brown everywhere else, and his underparts are streaked. The adult female and young are brown only (no red), and streaked over their entire bodies. The male juveniles will acquire their adult coloring by the first fall. All House Finches have short, cone-shaped bills.

Similar species: The male House Finch can be easily confused with several other finch species. The only one occurring in the Inland Empire is the Purple Finch, and it is a rare-to-uncommon winter visitor.

Variation in color of House Finch male

Unfortunately, it's not so simple with the female House Finch. At first sight, she can be easily confused with a female House Sparrow, since they are a similar size, shape, and color. But if you look closely, you will see the streaking on the breast of the female House Finch and an unstreaked breast on the female House Sparrow. The female

House Finch could also be confused with a female or immature Brown-headed Cowbird, but the Cowbird young are larger and have no streaking on their backs. In the winter, the female and juvenile House Finch could be confused with the immature White-crowned Sparrow. (See **Look-alikes** pages for comparisons with these other species).

Behaviors: House Finches are highly sociable, living in groups of as many as twenty-five, sometimes more. Because of this, they are not very territorial. They can be seen perched in the tops of trees and on telephone lines.

Voice: The male sings a bubbly, warbling song consisting primarily of three notes sung over and over. It even sings while flying. The male, female, and young all make a continual "wheat" call.

Nesting: House Finches are considered semicolonial nesters; their territories barely extend beyond their nests. They will build nests just about anywhere: in tree cavities, in old nests of other species, under eaves, in dead palm fronds that form a thatch along the trunk, and even in potted plants you may have hanging on your porch. The nests are usually only five to seven feet above the ground, although this can vary. The nests have been known to be parasitized by the Brown-headed Cowbird.

The female builds the nest of grasses, leaves, and other soft materials. She then lays four to five speckled blue-white eggs. The nests have an unclean appearance since the parents do not carry away the waste of their nestlings as other birds do.

Food: House Finches eat mainly weed seeds, but they will also eat buds, blossoms, and ripening fruit and berries.

Will they use my yard? Chances are great that they will. They are habituated to humans and live anyplace we do. Often they are the most common bird in a suburban area. You'd be hard-pressed to *not* have them in your yard! They are abundant in the Inland Empire and can be found feeding on lawns, in fruit trees, and at feeders. They don't like tall grasses or dense shrubbery. They especially love sunflower seeds and will often monopolize a feeder that has them.

Key things to look for:
1) Sparrow-sized. **2)** Male: red (sometimes orange or yellow) on the head, breast, and rump. **3)** Female: streaking overall and especially on the breast.

American Robin

Turdus migratorius

Spanish name: Zorzal petirrojo

American Robin adult

When can I expect to see them?
American Robins are common throughout North America and are known as harbingers of spring in the East, since they return every year when the temperatures warm. Robins in the Inland Empire are permanent residents and can be seen throughout the year. However, there are many more Robins here in the winter; it is thought that Robins that breed farther north winter here.

What do they look like? Robins are the largest North American thrush, being 9 to 11 inches in length. Both males and females are gray-brown above, with darker heads (although the females' may be lighter) and tails. The bills are yellow. In the male, the underparts are brick red; the female is paler. Both have white lower bellies. The juveniles have breasts that are cinnamon in color and heavily speckled with brown.

Similar species: There are no similar species that occur in the Inland Empire, other than the Western Bluebird, which is smaller, has a blue back and wings, and is here only in the winter.

Behaviors: Robins often run along the ground in search of food, in a run-stop-run pattern. Robins roost in large communal roosts (except during breeding season) and form large social flocks in winter months, feeding together during the day.

Various aspects of Robin behavior are still a mystery. For one thing, only males sing, but unlike most other birds, they do not sing in association with specific aspects of life, such as attracting a mate or advertising a territory. Robins sing early and late in the day, and they appear to sing most frequently just before the young hatch. Another mystery is that no specific courtship behaviors have been observed; therefore, no one knows exactly how they form pairs.

Voice: Songs are liquidy and in three or more phrases. "Cheeriup, cheerily, cheeriup," is repeated after a short pause. The male and female also give a short, shrill "teek" call in situations of possible danger; the call is often accompanied by a tail flick.

Nesting: The nest is placed on a horizontal limb or building, five to thirty feet above ground. It is made of grass, a middle layer of mud, and a lining of grasses. The female does the majority of the nest building. Her breast is actually used to form the nest; she sits in the nest and presses against the edges, often causing her breast to be mud-stained.

The Robin is one of the earliest birds to nest. It nests in open, suburban areas, on evergreens, in sturdy shrubs, and on horizontal constructed surfaces. The female does all the incubating; however, both parents feed the nestlings.

Food: Robins gather worms and insects from lawns in the spring. Because these birds have a habit of cocking their heads to the side, people once thought they were actually listening for worms and bugs. It is now known that this is not the case; robins use sight to locate and catch their prey. They also feed on berries, larger fruits, and some seeds in winter.

American Robin juvenile

Will they use my yard? Robins prefer those suburban areas that have larger expanses of lawn, in addition to trees appropriate for nesting and water nearby. They also love yards with berry-producing shrubs and trees.

Key things to look for:
1) Robin-sized. **2)** Gray backs and red breasts. **3)** Run-stop-run pattern along the ground.

Northern Flicker

Colaptes auratus cafer

Spanish name: Carpintero collarejo

People also refer to them as Red-shafted Flickers and Common Flickers.

When can I expect to see them? Northern Flickers are year-round residents in the Inland Empire, but they are more common in the winter. During the breeding season, they are not birds you would probably see very often in your yard, unless you live near the Santa Ana River.

What do they look like? Northern Flickers are larger than Robins, 12½ to 14 inches long. They have brown bars on the back and brownish spotted underparts, with a black bib. Like all woodpeckers, they have stiff tails, four toes (two pointed forward and two backward), short legs, and strong bills. The male and female basically look alike, with brown crowns and gray faces and no red on the back of the head. The male, however, has a red mustache stripe that the female lacks.

Two distinct groups occur. The Yellow-shafted Flicker occurs in the East. The group we have in the West is referred to as the Red-shafted Flicker. Two of the best identifying characteristics can be seen when they fly: they have large white rumps, and the undersurfaces of the Red-shafted Flicker's wings and tail are a light salmon red.

Similar species: The Flicker is brown, unlike the other woodpeckers in our area.

Behaviors: What makes Flickers unique among woodpeckers is their habit of feeding on the ground much of the time, rather than in a tree.

Flickers have a strong, undulating flight.

Flickers, as well as many other bird species, squash ants and preen themselves with them, since the ants contain a formic acid that helps control the small parasites living on the birds. This process is called anting.

Voice: Northern Flickers are noisy, frequently giving their loud calls, which include a rapid "wicka-wicka-wicka" and a single loud, drawn-out "keer." The males have no real song.

Nesting: During courtship, the Flickers will use branches, telephone poles, or whatever resonating material they can find as a drumming platform to announce their territory.

Northern Flicker female   *Northern Flicker male*

Northern Flickers nest in cavities they excavate, usually in live trees, although they will use dead trees, telephone poles, or fence posts. Flickers will use nest boxes, also, if the entrance hole is large enough. They have been known to enlarge the holes themselves! Their nest cavities can be taken over by Starlings, which are more aggressive and competitive.

The male chooses the nest site and does most of the excavating, which takes about one to two weeks. No extra material is added, other than fresh chips.

The female typically lays six to eight white eggs, and both adults incubate them, the male usually at night, for about two weeks. Both parents tend the nestlings, feeding them by regurgitation. The male broods the young for the first three weeks. As they get older, the nestlings stick their heads out of the cavity entrance to grab food from the adults. The young leave the nest in about four weeks.

Food: Flickers' favorite food is ants, and they can most often be seen on the ground, hopping about lawns and open spaces, probing for ants. Flickers also eat other insects and some berries.

Will they use my yard? Northern Flickers can be seen in suburban yards, most often on the ground or in large trees. They are shy, so they may be in your yard without your even being aware of them. Northern Flickers have been found to consume more ants in a yard if they are given suet. They will also come to feeders to eat bread, peanut butter mixture, etc.

Key things to look for:
1) A brown woodpecker. **2)** Salmon red under the wings when it flies.
3) A white rump.

Red-Shouldered Hawk

Buteo lineatus

Spanish name: Aguililla pechirroja

When can I expect to see them? Red-shouldered Hawks are actually fairly common in the Inland Empire and are permanent, year-round residents.

What do they look like? Red-shouldered Hawks are about the same size as Red-tailed Hawks (17 to 24 inches), but they are much more slender-looking, with somewhat longer tails and wings. As in most hawks, the male is smaller than the female. Other than that, the male and female look alike, with brown backs and dark reddish underparts, including the throat, thighs, and tail. The adults have dark tails barred with narrow white bands and dark wings with white barring. This gives them a black-and-white, checkerboard appearance. You can't always see the red shoulder that gives them their name.

Immatures look similar to adults, but their underparts are heavily streaked with brown (rather than barred), and they have little or no red shoulder patches. See **Look-alikes** pages for comparison.

Similar species: The Red-shouldered Hawk can be easily confused with the other two common hawk species in our area. The Cooper's Hawk lacks the red shoulders, and the banding on its tail is less distinct. When flying, the Cooper's Hawk stays low compared to the Red-shouldered. The Cooper's has white undertail coverts that are usually visible.

Red-shouldered Hawk adult

The immature Red-tailed Hawk has less distinct banding on the tail and lacks the reddish underparts of the Red-shouldered.

Behaviors: The Red-shouldered is a high-flying hawk, rather than low-flying like the

Cooper's Hawk. When it is perched, as on a telephone line, the Red-shouldered Hawk has a posture different from that of the Red-tailed Hawk. The Red-shouldered Hawk appears to have its head pulled into its shoulders, which are more rounded than those of the Red-tailed Hawk.

Voice: The pair is noisy during breeding season. The two repeatedly call a rapid "kee-you, kee-you, kee-you."

Nesting: The pair is faithful to its nesting territory year after year. Courtship is in late winter, and the female begins laying by March or April. The female lays two blotched eggs, and both sexes incubate. After about one month, the young hatch, and both parents tend them. The young leave the nest when they are a little over one month old, 35 to 42 days.

Food: Red-shouldered Hawks feed primarily on small mammals but will also take rabbits, opossums, skunks, and an occasional bird, snake, lizard, or large insect.

Will they use my yard? It is unlikely that you will see Red-shouldered Hawks in your yard, unless you have a wooded property and you live close to a creek or along the Santa Ana River.

Key things to look for:
1) Hawk with rounded wings, long tail. **2)** Distinct banding on the tail. **3)** Red shoulder patches. **4)** Black and white "checkered" upperparts.

Red-shouldered Hawk immature   *Red-shouldered Hawk immature*

Red-Tailed Hawk

Buteo jamaicensis

Spanish name: Aguililla colirroja

When can I expect to see them? Red-tailed Hawks are year-round residents of southern California. In the winter their numbers may increase due to an influx of migrating birds from colder regions.

What do they look like? Red-tailed Hawks are probably what most people think of when they think of a hawk. They are one of the largest hawks, from 19 to 25 inches long, with the female being slightly larger than the male (as is the case with most raptors). The male and female have similar coloration and shape; they are chunky, broad-winged, and short-tailed. The adults have distinctive red tails that are most visible when they are soaring. They also have a "belly band" between their light-colored chests and stomachs. Occasionally, you can see the black, or melanistic, phase of the Red-tailed.

The immature has the same body, wing, and tail shape, but the tail is brown and banded. The upperparts are somewhat mottled with white, and the breast is usually white. The underparts are more streaked and spotted than on the adult. The immature maintains this coloration for the first year of its life.

Similar species: The other two hawks in the Inland Empire, the Cooper's and the Red-shouldered Hawk, are less commonly seen. The Cooper's Hawk is smaller but could be confused with an immature Red-tailed. The Cooper's tail is longer and straighter (not the wedge shape of the Red-tailed), and they have distinct white undertail coverts. The immature Red-shouldered Hawk is similar in size to the Red-tailed, but with a slighter build. It has more variable dark streaking on the underparts and has white bars on the tail (rather than the brown bands of the Red-tailed).

Red-tailed Hawk adult

Red-tailed Hawk immature

Behaviors: Red-tailed Hawks soar high in the sky and, during the day-time, are among the easiest birds to spot. During breeding season you can often see them being harassed by other birds, especially crows, as they swoop and dive to get away.

Red-tailed Hawks have been persecuted by humans, and they are usually leery of us. They are often accused of killing chickens and other fowl, even though that is rarely true.

Voice: The most familiar call is the hoarse, rasping scream, sounding like "keeeeer," heard in many TV commercials and movies.

Nesting: Red-tailed Hawks build large stick nests in tall trees, such as eucalyptus and sycamore. They use their same nests year after year. They pair for life. If one of the pair dies, the survivor takes another mate.

The nesting season begins in January, during which time Red-tailed Hawks perform quite interesting aerial courtship displays that include much screaming.

The female lays two to three dull white eggs. The female is larger, since she does most of the incubating. The male feeds her while she is on the nest. Red-tailed Hawks are very protective at the nest and have been known to dive at people who get too close. The eggs hatch after about a month. Both adults feed the nestlings. When almost ready to fledge, the young will walk about the nest, stretching and flapping vigorously. The nestlings fledge about a month and a half after hatching. The young then follow the adults, squawking for food and learning the basics of catching it.

Food: Red-tailed Hawks eat primarily small rodents, although they will eat snakes, rabbits, and insects. They will also eat larger ground-dwelling birds, such as quail and meadowlarks. The Red-tailed Hawk has binocu-lar vision, which gives it superb sight for catching small prey from a great distance away.

Will they use my yard? Red-tailed Hawks are more likely to be seen in your yard if you have tall trees for nesting and open space nearby for for-aging. They are probably the most common raptor in the area. You can often see them on top of telephone poles next to the freeways or soaring slowly overhead.

Key things to look for:
1) Large hawk. **2)** Rounded wings. **3)** Soars high in the sky.
4) Adult: red tail. **5)** Immature: streaked underneath and striped on tail.

GREEN ACCENTS

Costa's Hummingbird

Calypte costae

Spanish name: Colibrí de Costa

When can I expect to see them? Costa's Hummingbirds are fairly common spring and summer breeders in the Inland Empire. They are becoming increasingly common here as permanent residents. Originally, they were found in desert oases, but they have expanded their range into more urbanized areas of southern California due to the increased availability of food.

What do they look like? The Costa's Hummingbird is the smallest hummingbird that occurs in our area, being 3¼ inches long. The male has a purple crown and throat whose feathers extend beyond the neck (called a gorget). The male and female are dingy white underneath, with green metallic upperparts.

Similar species: The Anna's Hummingbird male is larger and has a red, rather than purple, crown and throat, and darker underparts. The Black-chinned Hummingbird male also has purple on the throat, but the purple does not extend beyond the neck, and there is no purple on the crown. The female Costa's is whiter below than the Black-chinned Hummingbird female, although they are often indistinguishable. The female Anna's is slightly larger and darker underneath, usually with some patch of color on the throat. (See **Look-alikes** pages for comparison.)

Behaviors: The male Costa's has an elaborate courtship display. He flies in a U-shaped pattern into the air, rising as high as one hundred feet. He passes over the female and plunges downward with a continuous shrill whistle.

Costa's Hummingbird male

Photo by Charles Melton

Voice: The male's song is a loud "zing." The call of the Costa's Hummingbird is a series of high, metallic "tink" sounds, often made while feeding.

Nesting: The Costa's Hummingbird is known to breed in our area as early as February. Like all of our hummingbirds, the male Costa's is only involved in fertilizing the eggs; the female builds the nest and raises the young. She usually builds the nest within two to nine feet of the ground, in bushes, small trees, or weedy plants, avoiding dense, leafy trees. She makes a loosely built nest of fine plant fibers held together with spider-webs. The rim and interior are usually lined with small feathers. The Costa's nest is often indistinguishable from the Anna's Hummingbird nest.

The female Costa's lays two white eggs, about two days apart. She incubates, starting with the laying of the first egg, for about two weeks. The young are born tiny and altricial but are ready to fledge in about three weeks. It is thought that they only have one brood a year.

Food: As all of our hummingbirds do, the Costa's hovers before flowers to feed on the nectar. They also feed on insects and spiders.

Will they use my yard? Costa's Hummingbirds can be seen, increasingly, in suburban Inland Empire yards that provide plants with hummingbird flowers and open areas interspersed with trees. Costa's Hummingbirds are also attracted to hummingbird feeders placed out in the yard.

Key things to look for:
1) Very tiny hummingbird. **2)** Male: purple crown and purple feathers extending beyond the neck.

Costa's Hummingbird female   Photo by Charles Melton

Black-Chinned Hummingbird

Archilochus alexandri

Spanish name: Colibrí barbinegro

When can I expect to see them? Black-chinned Hummingbirds only show up in the Inland Empire during the months of April through September. While here, they breed. In the winter they migrate south to Mexico and Central America.

What do they look like? Both male and female Black-chinned Hummingbirds are metallic green above. The male has a violet band at the lower border of his black throat, although this is usually only seen in good light. The male has white underparts with green sides and flanks. The female is entirely white below, or may have faint greenish streaks on her throat. Both sexes have white spots just behind the eye (but good luck seeing them!). The immatures look almost indistinguishable from the females. However, the immature males may begin showing violet on the lower throat in early fall.

Similar species: The females and immatures of all three of our hummingbird species are difficult to tell apart, as the differences are often subtle. Look at the great similarities on the **Look-alikes** pages, but don't

Black-chinned Hummingbird male

Black-chinned Hummingbird female

Black-chinned Hummingbird female on nest

worry about telling them apart! The two best ways to separate the female Black-chinned and the Anna's are time of year and the nest. The Black-chinned Hummingbird's nest is very smooth on the outside and looks like it is made of nothing but fine spiderwebs. It is a light tan or gray.

The male Black-chinned, Costa's, and Anna's Hummingbirds are difficult to tell apart in poor light. Look at the throat to see if the color extends down the sides of the neck at all. If it does, then it is an Anna's. The purple patch on the male Costa's throat is larger, extending beyond the neck, than on the other two species.

Behaviors: The most amazing behavior of the tiny Black-chinned Hummingbird is its migration from the tropics of Central America to the western United States. It travels thousands of miles to nest!

Voice: The Black-chinned Hummingbird's call is a soft "tchew"; it also has a chase note of high squeals and the soft "tchew." Unlike the male Anna's, the male Black-chinned Hummingbird does not have a song.

Nesting: As with the other hummingbirds, the male's only involvement is in fertilizing the eggs. The female builds the nest, incubates, and raises the young. She often has two to three broods per year.

The nest is a tiny round cup made of plant down and occasionally other materials. It is held together by spiderwebs. It takes the female several days to complete a nest. The female lays two tiny white eggs and incubates them for about two weeks. The young remain in the nest, after hatching, for about three weeks. The nest is elastic and stretches as the nestlings grow.

Food: The Black-chinned Hummingbird feeds principally on the nectar of flowers, especially red ones. It will also eat pollen and insects, and it will dart out from a perch like a flycatcher to catch insects. Like all hummingbirds, the Black-chinned will come to a feeder with sugar water.

Will they use my yard? The Black-chinned Hummingbird is most likely to be seen in yards that offer large shade trees or in neighborhoods close to riparian areas or canyons. It can also be attracted to your yard if you provide hummingbird feeders and nectar-producing plants.

Key things to look for:
1) Small hummingbird. **2)** Metallic green back and head. **3)** The purple on the throat of the male does not extend down the side of the neck at all.

Anna's Hummingbird

Calypte anna

Spanish name: Colibrí de Anna

When can I expect to see them? The Anna's Hummingbird occurs year-round in the Inland Empire and is our most common hummingbird.

What do they look like? The Anna's Hummingbird is tiny, only 4 inches in length. The male is recognizable by his bright red head and throat, iridescent in sunlight but otherwise blackish. The female usually shows some flecks or a patch of red on her throat. Both sexes have metallic green backs and grayish underparts, washed with some green. They have needle-like bills. The young have shorter bills, and they lack any red on their throats. The immatures look similar to the females, with specks of red on their throats. The male immatures may show some red on their heads also.

Similar species: Black-chinned and Costa's Hummingbird males can be confused with the Anna's males if seen in a poor light where you can't distinguish the red and purple. The females and immatures of all three species are very similar. Study the **Look-alikes** pages to see the differences.

Don't worry about separating the females at this point! One of the best ways of telling a female Anna's from a Black-chinned is by the nest she builds. The Anna's nest looks much rougher than the Black-chinned Hummingbird's, being finished on the outside with plant and lichen pieces.

Behaviors: The males are very territorial and aggressive. You can often see a male perched on a small branch, waiting to swoop down on any intruding male hummingbird. They are often curious and will hover near your hat, face, or clothing, especially if you have red on.

Voice: The male's song is a series of rapid, thin squeaks. He sings perched or in flight. The male and female both utter a one-note "click" call when they feed or move between flowers.

Nesting: The male has an elaborate courtship display, which he performs for a female as she sits quietly in a tree or bush (or which he uses to intimidate other males). He climbs high in the sky, almost out of sight, and then plunges quickly toward the ground. He makes a "peek" sound with his wings just before reaching the ground and starting his climb upward again. He hovers at the top of his ascent, giving his squeaky song. This display is repeated many times.

The male is only involved in fertilizing the eggs; the female constructs the nest, incubates the eggs, and raises the young. She builds a tiny cup-shaped nest of plant down held together with spiderwebs and lined with feathers and fine down. She may build this nest anywhere from two feet off the ground to thirty feet high in a tree or shrub. If you are lucky enough to watch a female building her nest, you will see her sit in the nest and turn, weaving the spiderweb into it.

Anna's Hummingbirds begin nesting as early as January (before the arrival of migrant hummingbirds), but mostly from February to mid-May. They lay two tiny white eggs and incubate them for about two weeks. As the young grow, the nest stretches to accommodate their increase in size, until they are ready to fly at about 18 to 21 days. A female Anna's will have two broods a year and may even begin building a second nest while she is still feeding the young at the first nest!

Anna's Hummingbird male

Anna's Hummingbird female on nest

Anna's Hummingbird female
Photo by Charles Melton

Food: Anna's Hummingbirds feed primarily on nectar from reddish, tube-shaped flowers: "hummingbird flowers." They can hover as they feed and can fly backwards, up and down, and sideways, just like a helicopter. They also eat insects and spiders and feed insects (high in protein) to young in the nest.

Will they use my yard? The Anna's is present in virtually every type of yard, from dense apartment complexes to large, spacious lots. Anna's, like all our hummingbirds, can easily be attracted to a feeder full of sugar water, as well as to plants that have tubular, nectar-producing flowers.

Key things to look for:
1) Tiny. **2)** Long, needlelike bill. **3)** Red on the head and throat (only partial on throat if female). **4)** Rapid wingbeats that make a humming noise.

BLACK (IRIDESCENT)

Brown-Headed Cowbird
Molothrus ater

Spanish name: Vaquero cabecicafé

When can I expect to see them? Some Brown-headed Cowbirds are year-round residents of the Inland Empire, but most spend fall and winter in large flocks in agricultural areas of California's Central Valley. They are easier to see in the Inland Empire in the winter than at other times of year, due to their flocking habits.

What do they look like? Brown-headed Cowbirds are slightly larger and thinner than sparrows. The male has a metallic green-black body with a coffee brown head (the color can only be seen in good light). The female is dark brown above and paler brown below, with streaking. The juvenile is paler than the female overall and more heavily streaked below; the feathers on the wings and back have more of a scaled look. Young males molt to adult plumage in the late summer and begin showing patches of brown and iridescent green-black.

Similar species: Brown-headed Cowbirds are the same size and shape as Brewer's Blackbirds, but the Brewer's male has a yellow eye and thinner bill. The males could be confused with Starlings, but the Cowbirds have longer tails.

The females could be confused with females of various other species: a female House Finch (which is smaller), a female Brewer's Blackbird (which has a slightly larger, thinner bill), a California Towhee (which has no streaks), and female Sparrows (which are smaller). See the **Look-alikes** pages.

Brown-headed Cowbird female

Brown-headed Cowbird male

Behaviors: The most prominent behavior is discussed below under "Nesting."

Voice: The male's song is bubbly and sounds like a series of gurgles whose pitch goes up as it sings, sounding like "glug-glug-glee." The Brown-headed Cowbird also has a high, squeaky whistle in flight and a "chuck" call.

Nesting: The Brown-headed Cowbird is a nest parasite: it lays its eggs in the nest of a songbird. The Cowbird may lay as many as thirty eggs in the nests of other birds each nesting season! The choice of nest or host species is not well understood, but scientists have recorded that Brown-headed Cowbirds have parasitized over 220 species. In your yard, it would be most common to find a Cowbird laying its eggs in the nest of a House Finch.

The adult songbird raises the young of the Cowbird, which are often much larger than itself, as its own. The female Cowbird, when laying her eggs, may even remove eggs of the songbird. The Cowbird young usually hatch a day or two before the songbird young, which gives the Cowbirds a head start. Being larger and noisier, they get more food from the "parents." Some larger species, such as the Robin and Oriole, defend against Cowbird parasitism by abandoning their nests, covering the eggs, and starting new nests, or tossing the eggs from the nest.

A female Cowbird will lay up to thirty eggs per season in multiple nests, thereby reducing the survival rate of the young of other species. The Cowbird has had a tremendous impact on songbirds, pushing some species to the point of serious decline.

Food: Brown-headed Cowbirds eat mainly insects. Grasshoppers are their favorite food. They will also eat weed seeds, corn, wheat, oats, and some berries. They can be seen feeding on insects in your lawn or compost pile. They are especially attracted to areas with cattle, horses, or sheep. Cowbirds feed on insects in manure and on waste grain.

Will they use my yard? Cowbirds can be observed in any yard, especially during the breeding season. You may see them perched on telephone wires, looking for potential nest "victims." Since you wouldn't want to attract them to your yard, the best thing to do is *not* provide corn and oats at your feeder, since they are attracted to these foods.

Key things to look for:
1) Male: black bird, larger and thinner than a sparrow, thinner bill.
2) Female: larger and thinner than a sparrow, brownish overall.

Phainopepla

Phainopepla nitens

Spanish name: Capulinero negro

When can I expect to see them? In the Inland Empire, the Phainopepla can be seen most of the year only along the Santa Ana River, where it is uncommon. It is here in larger numbers, but still uncommon, from early April to early September, during its breeding season.

What do they look like? The Phainopepla is the only North American member of the Silky Flycatcher family. It has soft, silky plumage. The male's plumage is shiny black, and the female's is gray. Both sexes have red eyes, distinct crests, long tails, and white wing patches that can be seen when they fly.

Similar species: The only other similar-sized black bird is the Brewer's Blackbird, which has a yellow eye and no crest. The female Phainopepla could be confused with a Mockingbird, especially when flying. Upon a closer look, you will see the crest and red eye of the Phainopepla.

Behaviors: Phainopeplas often perch on the tops of shrubs.

Voice: The Phainopepla gives a low, one-note whistle that sounds like someone trying to get your attention. The male has a soft, short warble song that is rarely heard.

Phainopepla female

Nesting: The Phainopepla often has its first brood in a nearby mesquite or desert wash, then moves into the Inland Empire in the spring to raise a second brood. In the Inland Empire, it will nest in trees or shrubs. Both adults help build the open-cup nest made of twigs, plant down, and leaves bound together with spiderwebs. The female lays two to three grayish eggs splotched with black. Both parents incubate for about two weeks. When the eggs hatch, both parents care for the nestlings. The young fledge in about three weeks.

Food: The Phainopepla's favorite food is mistletoe berries, which are found in scrub areas. When they are nesting in more suburban areas, Phainopeplas eat insects, which they catch on the wing.

Phainopepla male

Will they use my yard? The Phainopepla is primarily a bird of desert washes and scrub, but it will nest in trees of yards that are at the urban-wildland interface, such as near Box Springs. I once had a Phainopepla visit my birdbath in the winter when I lived near Mt. Rubidoux.

Key things to look for:
1) Crested head.
2) White wing patches visible when they fly. **3)** Red eyes.
4) Male: shiny black plumage.
5) Female: darkish gray plumage.

European Starling

Sturnus vulgaris

Spanish name: Estornino Europeo

When can I expect to see them? The European Starling was introduced into New York around one hundred years ago by someone wanting to have one of every type of bird that occurs in Shakespeare's plays! Within sixty years, the Starling extended its range to include the entire United States. It is now a common, permanent resident and breeder of the Inland Empire.

What do they look like? Starlings are basically chunky, dark, fairly large birds with short tails and wings. The male and female look alike and have both a breeding (spring) plumage and a slightly different fall and winter nonbreeding plumage. In the winter they are dark with speckles over much of their bodies, and their bills are dark. In the spring the bills turn yellow and their bodies take on a green-black iridescence.

The young are gray-brown above and paler below with brown bills.

Similar species: The Brown-headed Cowbird and Brewer's Blackbird could be confused with the Starling, especially in poor lighting. The Cowbird and Blackbird have longer tails and shorter bills. They will not have the speckled feathers that the Starling has in winter.

Behaviors: Starlings are aggressive, gregarious, and very adaptable. They are known as habitat generalists. They feed and roost in large, noisy flocks.

European Starling adult in breeding plumage

Although both male and female Starlings have a distinct breeding plumage, they do not acquire it through molting, as most birds do. Instead, they actually lose their speckles by abrasion. Normal day-to-day wear causes the black iridescent parts of the feathers to be visible. Starlings only have a complete molt after the breeding season is over.

Voice: Starlings have a large repertoire of "tunes" within their call, including whistles, clicks, squeaks, and twitterings. They even incorporate pieces of other birds' songs. They have a short "chjjj" flight call.

Nesting: Starlings are very aggressive nesters, often nesting in cavities and taking over nest sites from native species, such as bluebirds, woodpeckers, and flickers. They occasionally nest in loose colonies, laying synchronously. Their territory does not extend much beyond the nest hole.

Food: You can often see Starlings walking energetically over grassy lawns. They feed on the ground, on beetles, caterpillars, grasshoppers, millipedes, and other insects. They are also attracted to figs and other fruit, garbage, snails, and weed seeds. In other words, they are omnivores.

Will they use my yard? Starlings especially like yards that have a lot of lawn, and therefore a lot of insects, and yards that provide nesting cavities, including nest boxes if the holes are large enough. If at all possible, try to keep these birds out of your yard, since they are considered a pest species to native cavity nesters. To discourage them, don't put oats or peanut hearts at your feeding stations, since they especially like these foods. Also, be sure that the entrance hole to any nest box you build is less than 1½ inches in diameter. This is large enough to allow the birds you want, but too small for the Starlings to pass through.

Key things to look for:
1) Chunky body. **2)** Short tail. **3)** Longish, pointed bill. **4)** Speckles in winter. **5)** Large, noisy groups that make squeaky, whistly, twittering sounds.

European Starling adult in fall plumage   *European Starling juvenile*

Brewer's Blackbird

Euphagus cyanocephalus

Spanish name: Tordo de Brewer

When can I expect to see them? Brewer's Blackbirds are permanent year-round residents of the Inland Empire and can be seen at any time. They are more visible in the winter due to their flocking habits during this time.

What do they look like? The Brewer's Blackbird is just that, a Robin-sized, black bird, with a purplish gloss on its head and neck. The male has a distinctly yellow eye. The female and juveniles are gray-brown overall and have brown eyes.

Similar species: The male could be confused with a Brown-headed Cowbird male. However, the Brewer's Blackbird is slightly larger, with a longer tail, and has the glossy head and the yellow eye. It could also be confused with a European Starling, which has a short tail and stubby body.

The female Brewer's Blackbird is an overall brown bird that can be confused with the California Towhee, the European Starling, and the female Brown-headed Cowbird. See the **Look-alikes** pages.

Behaviors: The Brewer's Blackbird is a gregarious bird that often appears in large flocks in the winter with European Starlings and Brown-headed Cowbirds. When feeding, the Brewer's Blackbird can be separated from other species in the flock by its posture; it usually holds its tail pointed slightly downward.

Brewer's Blackbird female

Voice: The male's song is a short, soft, creaky "que-ee." The calls are a variety of whistles and clucks, ranging from high (and somewhat piercing) to a dry, hard sound.

Nesting: Brewer's Blackbirds are semicolonial nesters, nesting in groups of usually three to twenty pairs. They are frequent hosts to the Brown-headed Cowbird. They nest on the ground in thick, weedy cover, or in shrubs. The nests are sturdy, built of twigs and grasses. The female builds the nest and lays four to six blotched eggs. She does all the incubating, for about two weeks. The male guards the nest. The males may be polygamous, having two (or more) mates at once. The young leave the nest about two weeks after hatching.

Food: The Brewer's Blackbird walks along the ground in short jerks and stops as it searches for grasshoppers, crickets, caterpillars, seeds, grain, and fruit.

Will they use my yard? Human settlement has greatly increased the distribution of the Brewer's Blackbird. They have invaded cities, suburbs, and agricultural areas due to increases in food supply and appropriate nesting sites. So yes, they will probably appear in your yard at some time, especially if you provide cracked corn and millet.

Key things to look for:
1) Robin-sized. **2)** Long tail. **3)** Slim bill. **4)** Female: brown overall.
5) Male: glossy black, with yellow eye.

Brewer's Blackbird male

American Crow

Corvus brachyrhynchos

Spanish name: Cuervo Americano

When can I expect to see them? American Crows are year-round, permanent residents of urban and suburban areas of the Inland Empire. Their range has expanded tremendously in southern California due to human habitation. In the 1920s, Crows were actually considered a "novelty," appearing in only certain locales!

What do they look like? Crows are large (17½ inches long), all-black birds. The males and females look alike. The tail is straight and the bill is stout.

Similar species: The only species that Crows could be confused with is the Common Raven, which occurs much less frequently in urban areas. The Crow is smaller, and the tail shape is a distinguishing feature; it is straight in the Crow and wedge-shaped in the Raven. Also, the Crow's bill is much less stout than that of the Raven. The Crow does not soar as much as the Raven.

Behaviors: Many people consider Crows a nuisance. However, Crows (and Ravens) are considered to be some of the most intelligent birds, capable of learning. Crows tend to be wary of people, as they often have been persecuted.

Crows are gregarious and occur in raucous, organized flocks in the fall and winter. They will roost in flocks of up to one thousand in the fall and winter and then return to their year-round territories early each morning. Some flocks may fly up to fifty miles from the roost to feed each day! They fly back to the roost area along fixed flight lines. They have congregation areas where they meet before flying to roost.

Crows practice anting in a passive way. Rather than preening with ants, they will stand over an anthill and let the ants crawl all over them.

Voice: Crows have a number of calls, the most frequent of which is the familiar high, nasal "caw."

Nesting: Crows are two to three years old before they breed. They mate for life. They build their nests high in large trees, usually twenty to sixty feet above the ground. The nests are built of sticks, twigs, and bark strands. During nesting season you can see them moving slowly through dead branches, breaking off one at a time and carrying it to the nest. Researchers have found that, as Acorn Woodpeckers do, several generations of young Crows may help raise the nestlings.

Food: Crows are considered omnivores; in other words, they will eat just about anything. They stride along the ground in search of food, rather than hopping as most birds do. They will drop nuts from a high elevation onto the ground to break them open. They also eat the eggs and young of other bird species. They cache food.

Will they use my yard? The question is: If they aren't using your yard, why not? Even if you don't want to attract them to your yard, plan on them being there anyway! They have definitely benefited from urbanization. They are quite common in suburban areas with large trees and orchards.

Key things to look for:
1) Large. **2)** Black. **3)** Straight tail.

American Crow

Common Raven

American Crow

Common Raven

BLACK AND WHITE

Black-Throated Gray Warbler   *Dendroica nigrescens*

Spanish name: Chipe negrigrís

When can I expect to see them? Black-throated Gray Warblers migrate through the Inland Empire in spring and fall. They winter in Mexico. The peak of the spring migration is around mid-to-late April. The fall migration occurs over a more extended time frame, beginning in mid-August and extending into late October.

What do they look like? They are small, slender birds with thin beaks. The male has a black throat, cheek, and crown, gray upperparts, and white underparts. The female has a white throat streaked with black. She also has a slate-gray cheek and crown. Both sexes have a bright yellow spot in front of the eye, visible only at close range.

Similar species: The only species that occurs in the Inland Empire that might be confused with the Black-throated Gray Warbler is the White-crowned Sparrow, due to the Sparrow's black and white stripes. The black throat for which this bird is named distinguishes it from the Sparrow, which has a pale throat.

Black-throated Gray Warbler

Behaviors: The Black-throated Gray Warbler is not a shy bird and does not seem particularly concerned about having humans around.

Voice: The male's variable song is full of z's, sounding basically like "zeedle-zeedlezeedle-zeet."

Nesting: The Black-throated Gray Warbler nests mainly in mixed fir or pine forests in the western mountains.

Food: They are strictly insect eaters.

Will they use my yard? Black-throated Gray Warblers will use suburban yards during migration as they look for insects in the vegetation provided. They are fond of areas with oak trees and also areas with underbrush.

Key things to look for:
1) Small. **2)** Black throat. **3)** Black and white stripes on face.

Black Phoebe
Sayornis nigricans

Spanish name: Mosquero negro

When can I expect to see them? Black Phoebes are fairly common year-round residents of the Inland Empire, although some seasonal movement occurs.

What do they look like? The Black Phoebe is sparrow-sized, about 6¾ inches long. Both the male and the female have black heads, upperparts, tails, and breasts. The belly and undertail coverts are white. The juveniles have a different plumage only for a short time; they are browner, with two cinnamon wing bars and a cinnamon rump.

Similar species: The Dark-eyed Junco is the only bird that occurs in our area that could be confused with the Black Phoebe. However, the Junco is in the Inland Empire only in the fall and winter. In addition, the Junco feeds on the ground and does not flycatch like the Phoebe. It also does not have the tail-pumping behavior of the Phoebe.

Behaviors: Black Phoebes pump their tails up and down slowly as they perch.

Black Phoebe

Voice: The male Black Phoebe has a four-part song, a rising "pee-ee" followed by a descending "pee-ee." The two most commonly heard calls are a loud "tseee" and a sharper "tsip."

Nesting: The Black Phoebe prefers to nest near water, even if it is only a backyard fountain. The female builds the nest of mud and plant material, usually grass, and often places it under the eaves of a building or under a bridge. She usually lays four to six white eggs. Only the female incubates, for about two weeks. The nestlings are born altricial and remain in the nest for two to three weeks before fledging.

Food: Black Phoebes are insect eaters that feed close to the ground. They often catch insects from a low perch, such as a branch, a wall, or a mailbox, then alight on a different perch. They will continue this behavior over and over as they seize bees, ants, beetles, moths, flies, and caterpillars. They regurgitate small, round pellets of indigestible parts of large insects.

Will they use my yard? Black Phoebes will use yards if there is fresh water nearby (even swimming pools are used!) and if there is a lawn for catching insects. They may build their nest under the eaves of your house and will use this same nest from year to year.

Key things to look for:
1) Small black-and-white bird. **2)** Continually pumps its tail. **3)** Flies from perch to perch.

White-Crowned Sparrow   *Zonotrichia leucophrys*

Spanish name: Gorrión coroniblanco

When can I expect to see them? White-crowned Sparrows are winter visitors only, from the end of September until the middle of April.

What do they look like? The males are one of the most easily identified "little brown birds," due to the strong black-and-white striping on the head. The female's striping is slightly duller, and the stripes on the immatures' heads are more cinnamon brown and cream.

Similar species: Other than the head stripes, there is nothing to distinguish the White-crowned from any other small sparrow. The immatures can be easily confused with immature Golden-crowned Sparrows (not shown), which also occur in the Inland Empire in the winter but in much smaller numbers. But watch out! They can occur in mixed-species flocks. The immature White-crowned Sparrow will always have brown and cream stripes, with no hint of a yellow-gold central crown stripe (like the immature Golden-crowned). The black and white stripes of the Black-throated Gray Warbler could be confusing. However, the White-crowned Sparrow has a pale throat, not the black throat of the Warbler.

White-crowned Sparrow adult

Behaviors: White-crowned Sparrows feed in small-to-large groups while in the Inland Empire. They startle easily and flee to shrubs for safety.

Voice: During the winter, you will most often hear the White-crowned Sparrows making their soft "tzit" call. At times, the males will also give their distinctive song, which is usually one to two thin, whistled notes followed by a twittering trill.

Nesting: White-crowned Sparrows do not nest in the Inland Empire; they migrate to the coast or to higher elevations.

Food: The White-crowned Sparrow hops along the ground in search of weed or grass seeds and sometimes eats insects or catkins.

Will they use my yard? White-crowned Sparrows like yards that have open lawns surrounded by dense shrubs or tangles of vines to hide in. They can be attracted to ground feeders with sunflower seeds and nutmeats.

Key things to look for:
1) Sparrow size and shape. **2)** Black and white stripes on head.
3) Pale throat.

White-crowned Sparrow juvenile

Nuttall's Woodpecker

Picoides nuttallii

- -

Spanish name: Carpintero de Nuttall

When can I expect to see them? Since Nuttall's Woodpeckers are native to California and are Inland Empire residents, you can see them year-round. However, they are not regular visitors to yards, and you may only see (or hear) them occasionally, primarily during breeding season.

What do they look like? The Nuttall's Woodpecker is a black-and-white bird, 7 to 7½ inches long. Like all local woodpeckers, they have stiff tails and short legs with four toes, two pointed forward and two backwards. They have straight, hard, pointed bills that they use as chisels or hammers. The male has a black crown and the nape of the neck is red. The female looks just like the male, except she lacks the red nape.

Similar species: The other black-and-white woodpeckers the Nuttall's could be confused with in our area are the Downy (not discussed) and the Acorn Woodpecker. The Downy, less common in our area, is smaller, with a smaller bill and no spotted feathers on the sides. This is a good circumstance in which to learn your bird calls, since the Nuttall's, Downy, and Acorn Woodpeckers all sound very different.

Behaviors: Using their stiff tails for support, Nuttall's Woodpeckers "hop" up and around tree trunks in search of insects. Pairs remain on year-round territories.

Voice: Their call is a sharp, often rattling "pweek." They also have a high-pitched whinny. During breeding season, both the male and female drum on resonant timber or telephone poles as a territorial or courtship display. Like all woodpeckers, they have thick skulls and strong skull muscles that absorb the shock.

Nesting: They nest in cavities in dead trees or in dead limbs of deciduous trees, usually in riparian or oak woodlands. The male, with some help from the female, excavates the cavity, which is placed two to sixty feet above the ground. (They also roost in these cavities at night.) The female lays usually three to five white eggs, and both sexes incubate them for about two weeks, the male at night. The young are born altricial and are tended by both parents. They fledge about a month after hatching.

Nuttall's Woodpecker female

Nuttall's Woodpecker male

Food: The feeding "territories" of these birds are much larger than their nesting ones and may extend well into suburban areas. Nuttall's Woodpeckers feed primarily on insects found on the trunks and branches of trees. During their search for insects, they creep diagonally over the trunk, probing into crevices and flaking off bark rather than drilling. They listen for the sounds of the insects to help locate them.

Will they use my yard? Nuttall's Woodpeckers will most likely use your yard if you have large deciduous trees, such as sycamores, cottonwoods, willows, and oaks, where they can look for insects. You are more likely to see Nuttall's Woodpeckers if you live near areas like the Santa Ana River, Fairmount Park, Box Springs Mountain, Sycamore Canyon, or the University of California, Riverside. You can offer them suet with pieces of peanut or insects in it (you can purchase this or make your own).

Key things to look for:
1) Typical woodpecker. **2)** Black-and-white striped back. **3)** Props itself up with its stiff tail as it hunts for insects on the sides of tree branches.

Acorn Woodpecker
Melanerpes formicivorus

Spanish name: Carpintero arlequín

When can I expect to see them? Acorn Woodpeckers are year-round residents of the Inland Empire and are becoming increasingly common. They are highly sedentary unless forced to wander because their food supply is exhausted.

What do they look like? Acorn Woodpeckers are about Robin-sized, approximately 9 inches. They are known as the "clown bird," due to the black ring around their bills, their white cheeks and foreheads, and their red caps. The male and female look very similar, except the female has a black patch separating her white forehead from her red crown. In flight, you can see the white rump and small white patches on the outer wings of these birds.

Similar species: Northern Flickers have white rumps too, but they are larger and more brown and have red under their wings, visible when they fly. Nuttall's Woodpeckers have striped backs and black rumps.

Behaviors: Acorn Woodpeckers have a unique living arrangement. They live in year-round social groups of two to fifteen relatives, including one to four cobreeding sibling males and one to three cobreeding sibling females and their offspring from several previous years. Two to twelve birds sleep together in dormitory holes.

Acorn Woodpeckers store acorns in holes in dead trees, fence posts, and telephone poles, and they defend these granaries (see photo in **Attracting Birds to Your Yard**). They are highly territorial, defending a territory of oak and sap trees, granaries, nest holes, and dormitory holes.

They have an undulating flight, as all woodpeckers do.

Voice: When Acorn Woodpeckers are around, they are often conspicuous due to their loud, raucous vocalizations, though they can be very quiet if they are aware that people are nearby. They frequently make their calls, which include "wack-a, wack-a" and "kerack, kerack," when reconnecting with others in the group.

Nesting: Acorn Woodpeckers are known as "cooperative breeders": birds that are not the parents will provide care in rearing the young. Only one nest is active at any one time. The nest can be communal or contain the eggs of a single female. Nonbreeding helpers incubate, brood, and feed the nestlings. Helpers include yearlings and two-year-olds of both sexes, a larger proportion being female.

This social system allows females and males, unlike most birds, to breed in the same group that reared them. They avoid inbreeding, however, by not breeding until all possible parents of the opposite sex have moved to other territories or have died and been replaced by Acorn Woodpeckers from other groups.

Food: The primary winter food source for the Acorn Woodpecker in oak woodlands is known to be acorns, hence the name. They are dependent upon oak trees, plucking the acorns from the trees and then storing them in granaries for use by the entire social group during the winter or lean times. In more urban areas, such as Riverside, they also consume walnuts, pecans, and other nuts.

In the summer they eat large quantities of insects and are skillful aerial flycatchers. They drink sap from oak trees by drilling into the bark of a live tree and drinking from the little pits they have made. They also eat seeds and other nuts and some fruit.

Will they use my yard? You will be more likely to see Acorn Woodpeckers in your yard if you have oak trees or palms. They will also eat at feeders, if provided almonds, walnuts, and fruit.

Key things to look for:
1) Black-and-white bird. **2)** In a group. **3)** Call sounds like "wack-a, wack-a." **4)** White rumps and white in their wings visible when they fly.

Acorn Woodpecker female   *Acorn Woodpecker male*

BLACK AND ORANGE

Hooded Oriole

Icterus cucullatus

Spanish name: Bolsero cuculado

When can I expect to see them? It's always such a delight to see these beautiful birds return to my yard. I start looking for them in May, although they return as early as mid-March. They are considered spring and summer visitors and breeders, which means they will migrate south for the winter, usually by the end of September.

What do they look like? The Hooded Oriole is about the size of a Robin but more slender. It has a slender bill. The male is a spectacular combination of black and orange. The upper back, wings, and tail are black, in addition to the black extending from the eyes down to the throat and breast. The remainder of the male is a bright orange. There are two white wing bars.

The female is much duller, being olive-green above and yellow below, with dark gray wings and the two white wing bars. The immatures resemble the females, although the young males' throats begin to turn black by their first spring.

Similar species: The only other oriole that occurs commonly in the Inland Empire is the Bullock's Oriole. The male Bullock's has a black cap, rather than an orange hood.

The female Hooded Oriole and Bullock's Oriole look annoyingly alike. The Hooded Oriole female is more yellow overall than the female Bullock's Oriole, which has the lighter belly. (Hint: the easiest way to tell them apart is to see which male they're hanging out with! And then study the photos on the **Look-alikes** pages.)

Behaviors: Hooded Orioles are fairly shy birds and often stay in the dense foliage of shrubs and large trees; so in spite of the males' bright colors, they can often be hard to see (listening for their chatter helps).

Voice: The male has a warbly, throaty song of whistles and chatter. Both sexes have a sharp "wheat" call.

Nesting: Hooded Orioles nest almost exclusively in palm trees, although they have been known to nest in eucalyptus, willow, and ash. The female builds a cuplike nest sewn with fibers to the underside of a palm frond or overhanging leaves. The nest is lined with dried grasses and other soft materials. The female lays four eggs, usually pale yellow or blue and blotched or spotted with browns, purples, and grays. The female incubates the eggs for about two weeks. The nestlings leave the nest about two weeks after hatching. The male helps to feed the young, both in the nest and after they have fledged. Sometimes, Hooded Orioles will nest two or three times in one year.

Food: Hooded Orioles feed on insects, blossoms, and fruit. They often hang upside-down when searching for insects, as Bushtits do.

Will they use my yard? If you have palm trees nearby and fruit trees in your yard, you can pretty well plan on having Hooded Orioles in your yard. They feed on fruit and flowering trees (they love my apricots). They may come to an oriole or hummingbird feeder filled with sugar water.

Key things to look for:
1) Slender, Robin-sized. **2)** Male: orange hood. **3)** Female: yellow overall (belly the same color as the rest of her).

Hooded Oriole male

Hooded Oriole female

Hooded Oriole juvenile

Hooded Oriole female at the nest

Black-Headed Grosbeak
Pheucticus melanocephalus

Spanish name: Picogrueso tigrillo

When can I expect to see them? Black-headed Grosbeaks can be seen in the Inland Empire from early April into September. They often migrate through residential areas, favoring riparian woodlands for nesting, although they will nest in shrubs and trees in more wooded suburban yards.

Black-headed Grosbeak immature male

Black-headed Grosbeak male

Black-headed Grosbeak female

What do they look like? The Black-headed Grosbeak is 8 inches long, with a stout, conical bill. The male is conspicuous, with its cinnamon-orange underparts and black head and tail. The wings are black and white. A first-fall male is a rich buff below with no streaks.

The female has a brown back, tail, and wings, and a tan breast. She has a striped head and slightly streaked sides. Both males and females have yellow wing linings that can be seen in flight.

Similar species: The male Black-headed Grosbeak could be confused with two other birds, a Spotted Towhee male and a male Bullock's Oriole, being of similar size and color. However, the Grosbeak is chunkier and has a much more massive bill than the Oriole and Towhee. Also, the Towhee tends to be on the ground or concealed in small bushes, whereas the Grosbeak sings from the treetops.

The female and immature could be confused with Sparrow and Finch females and immatures, but the female is larger, with a more massive bill. Her yellow wing linings can be seen when she flies (see **Look-alikes** pages).

Behaviors: The Black-headed Grosbeak winters in Mexico.

Voice: The male Black-headed Grosbeak has a Robin-like song. The female also sings, although her song is less complex. They also have a sharp "peek" call.

Nesting: The nest is normally placed in the fork of a small tree, about four to twelve feet above ground. The female builds the bulky nest with twigs. Both parents incubate the three to four pale green eggs for about two weeks. Both sexes occasionally sing while sitting on the nest. The young remain in the nest for about two weeks before fledging.

Food: The Black-headed Grosbeak eats seeds from pines and other trees. They also eat fruit, buds, berries, and some insects.

Will they use my yard? The Black-headed Grosbeak can be found in yards that offer a variety of coniferous and deciduous trees. The Grosbeak is attracted to bird feeders offering sunflower and other seeds.

Key things to look for:
1) Smaller than a Robin. **2)** Yellow wing linings. **3)** Stout, conical bill.

Bullock's Oriole

Icterus bullockii

Spanish name: Bolsero de Bullock

Bullock's Orioles were previously called Northern Orioles.

When can I expect to see them? Some Bullock's Orioles are summer visitors in the Inland Empire, although most migrate through on their way to and from the local mountains where they breed. So the best time to see them is in the spring and fall.

What do they look like? The Bullock's Oriole male is a conspicuous, orange-and-black bird. It has a black upper back, a black patch under the throat, black wings with large white patches, an orange rump, and a black tail with large orange patches on the outer feathers. Its head is black on top with an orange face and a black eye line.

The female is olive-gray above, and the head and breast are a pale yellow. The tail is yellowish, the belly is whitish, and the wings have two white wing bars. The juveniles are similar to the females, although the juvenile males begin to take on the appearance of adult males during the first fall plumage, when their throats turn black.

Similar species: The male Bullock's Oriole could be confused with Hooded Oriole and Black-headed Grosbeak males, both also being orange and black. The male Hooded Oriole has an orange head and black under the chin, whereas the Bullock's Oriole has black on top of the head and under the chin, with orange on the cheeks. The Black-headed Grosbeak male has a black head also, but a much stouter body and bill. The Grosbeak also has yellow wing linings that can be seen during flight.

The female Bullock's and Hooded Orioles are very similar. The Bullock's Oriole female, however, has paler underparts than the Hooded female. (See **Look-alikes** pages for comparison.)

Behaviors: In spite of the colors, the Bullock's Oriole male can be missed as it searches vigorously for insects in the tops of tall trees. The female often blends with the leaves, making herself even more difficult to see.

Voice: The Bullock's Oriole chatters much like the Hooded Oriole does—both sexes do a lot of chattering. They also have an emphatic two-note "skip" call. The male's song is a four- to eight-part, medium-pitched whistle.

Bullock's Oriole adult male

Bullock's Oriole female

Bullock's Oriole, first year male

Nesting: The female skillfully weaves an oval-shaped bag, about six inches long, out of grasses and plant fibers, attaching it to twigs and branches at the rim or sides. She lays four to five pale gray or pale blue eggs with spots or squiggly dark lines. The female incubates the eggs for about two weeks. The young remain in the nest for about two weeks after hatching. The nests are frequently parasitized by Brown-headed Cowbirds. Both sexes vigorously defend the nest, eggs, and young against predators.

Food: Bullock's Orioles feed primarily on insects: caterpillars, beetles, leafhoppers, aphids, etc. They will eat fruit and drink nectar from flowers also.

Will they use my yard? You may be lucky enough to have one nesting in your yard if you have large deciduous trees. Bullock's Orioles may be attracted to yards with feeders. You can purchase feeders made specifically for orioles, or they may drink from hummingbird feeders. They also may be attracted if fruit is put out for them, especially orange halves.

Key things to look for:
1) Thin body and bill. **2)** Male: black and orange colors, black head.
3) Female: pale yellow with whitish belly.

GRAY

Ruby-Crowned Kinglet

Regulus calendula

Spanish name: Reyezuelo sencillo

When can I expect to see them? The Ruby-crowned Kinglet is primarily a winter visitor to the Inland Empire, although you can see them as early as mid-October and as late as mid-April. They do not nest in the Inland Empire.

What do they look like? Ruby-crowned Kinglets are tiny, plump birds, about 4¼ inches long—just slightly larger than an Anna's Hummingbird! The Kinglets are grayish olive above and dusky underneath, with two white wing bars. The male and female look alike, although the male does have a red crown patch that is rarely seen.

Similar species: The Ruby-crowned Kinglet is similar to a Bushtit. However, the Bushtit lacks the two white wing bars, is usually in a group, and is in the Inland Empire all year. The Kinglet can also be confused with an Orange-crowned Warbler, which occurs in the Inland Empire during winter. The Orange-crowned Warbler does not have wing bars and has a yellowish wash on the underparts.

Ruby-crowned Kinglet

Behaviors: The Ruby-crowned Kinglet is an active, nervous little bird that flits, like the Bushtit, through the trees and shrubs in yards.

Voice: You can hear the Ruby-crowned Kinglet give its scolding "je-dit, je-dit" call as it moves through the shrubs and trees. Compare it to the soft twittering of the Bushtit.

Nesting: Kinglets do not nest in the Inland Empire, but instead head north or to higher elevations to nest in the pines and firs. You may see them nesting in nearby mountains in May through July.

Food: Ruby-crowned Kinglets forage for insects, insect eggs, and larvae in shrubs, trees, and leaf litter on the ground. Because of their thin bills, Kinglets can reach insects that larger birds can't.

Will they use my yard? Kinglets will use any suburban yard that provides bushes, trees, and litter where they can find insects. Although Kinglets feed on insects primarily, they can be lured to feeding stations with suet, peanuts, and other cracked nuts. They are also attracted to birdbaths or other water sources.

Key things to look for:
1) Solitary. **2)** Two white wing bars. **3)** Tiny grayish green bird.
4) Here only in the winter.

Bushtit   *Psaltriparus minimus*

Spanish name: Sastrecí

They are also referred to as Common Bushtits.

When can I expect to see them? Bushtits are common year-round residents of the Inland Empire.

What do they look like? The Bushtit is only 4½ inches long. Both sexes look alike, with a plain gray back with light brown underparts and brown cheeks. The tail is long for the body size. The only difference is the eye color; males have brown eyes and females have yellow eyes. The male does not assume breeding plumage.

Similar species: They look similar to Ruby-crowned Kinglets and have similar feeding habits, but Kinglets are here only in the winter and do not move in groups.

Behaviors: Except when breeding, the Bushtits are highly gregarious and are always seen in loose family groups. You have to look quickly, as they are continuously on the move through trees and bushes, looking for insects. See if you can actually follow a group in its movement and count the number in the group. Good luck!

Bushtits are seldom disturbed by humans nearby and almost seem to be oblivious to us, except during nest building, when they may abandon their nests if disturbed.

Voice: The Bushtits' calls are very high, bell-like twitterings, made continually in order to maintain the group as the birds move through vegetation. The male has no real song.

Nesting: I think the Bushtits construct some of the prettiest nests. They make a hanging, gourd-shaped nest, woven around and supported by twigs. The nest is eight to ten inches long and made of grass, lichen, moss, and leaves secured by spiderwebs. The entrance hole is on the side, near the top.

The male and female both help build the nest. The rim is built first, and most of the remainder of the nest is built from the inside. The process is actually quite comical to watch: both male and female are in the nest, punching materials into place and twittering away! It takes them about two weeks to construct the nest.

Bushtit adult at nest   *Bushtit male*   Photo by Charles Melton

Both the male and female incubate the five to seven white eggs. They are known to be "cooperative breeders": the previous year's young are helpers at the nest. The young are born altricial and are tended by both parents. They leave the nest in about two weeks and become independent in another week.

Food: Bushtits feed on small insects, aphids, beetles, mealy bugs, leafhoppers, and spiders obtained from the foliage and twigs of woody plants. Bushtits are often seen hanging upside down under a leaf or on the end of a branch to feed. In the fall and winter they also eat plant material, the bulk of which is leaf galls.

Will they use my yard? Bushtits will use suburban yards, especially if there are adequate shrubs and small trees for nesting. They will visit backyard feeding stations during the winter and are especially fond of suet.

Key things to look for:
1) Tiny, gray bird with a long tail. **2)** Often in a group. **3)** Constantly moving and twittering. **4)** Often hangs upside down.

Warbling Vireo

Vireo gilvus

Spanish name: Víreo gorjeador

When can I expect to see them? The Warbling Vireo is only a migrant through the Inland Empire, and much more common here during spring than during fall migration.

What do they look like? This is one of the most nondescript gray birds there is, with no wing bars or eye ring. The Warbling Vireo has an inconspicuous whitish eyebrow line and a whitish breast and is about 5 inches long. Immatures are washed with yellow on the sides, flanks, and under the tail.

Similar species: Another nondescript bird is the Orange-crowned Warbler, which is olive green rather than gray, smaller, and has a thinner bill. Other gray birds include the larger Mockingbird and the smaller Bushtit. The Warbling Vireo feeds in a different manner than the Warblers and Bushtits, which flit and move about quickly. Warbling Vireos forage by moving slowly through the twigs and leaves, as if looking under each leaf carefully.

Warbling Vireo

Behaviors: Cowbirds often find and parasitize Vireo nests, possibly because male Vireos actually sing while at the nest.

Voice: In contrast to its drab coloring, the Warbling Vireo has a very colorful warbling song. Only the male sings, often while he is at the nest. Unfortunately, we here in the Inland Empire may not have the pleasure of hearing them, since the birds only migrate through. They also call a harsh, nasal, up-slurred note, often repeatedly.

Nesting: The Warbling Vireo nests in riparian woodlands at higher elevations and winters in Central America.

Food: Warbling Vireos are insect eaters primarily, but they also eat some berries.

Will they use my yard? Warbling Vireos could very well be in your yard without your ever knowing it. They are difficult to see, due to their total lack of distinctive plumage and their ability to blend with the leaves.

Key things to look for:
1) Gray. **2)** Nondescript. **3)** Slow foraging habit. **4)** Inconspicuous white eye line.

Western Screech Owl   *Otus megascops*

Spanish name: Tecolote occidental

When can I expect to see them? The Western Screech Owl is an uncommon permanent resident of the Inland Empire. It is losing habitat in southern California due to increased urbanization. It is nocturnal and may go unobserved even though it occurs year-round in our area.

What do they look like? This is a small owl, smaller than a Robin! The male and female look alike, being generally gray overall, with ear tufts and yellow eyes.

Similar species: There is no similar owl that occurs in the Inland Empire. The Great Horned Owl is almost three times larger.

Behaviors: Like other owls, Western Screech Owls fly silently as they hunt for food at night. They roost during the day in large trees and perch near the trunks. They regurgitate pellets of indigestible fur and bone. You

Western Screech Owl

can sometimes find the regurgitated pellets lying on the ground below their roosts or nests.

Voice: The typical call is a series of five to nine rapid one-note "hoots," reminiscent of a bouncing ball. Western Screech Owls also give a short trill followed by a rapid trill. This is sung in duet by the male and female.

Nesting: Western Screech Owls use cavities to nest, either natural cavities or those previously excavated by woodpeckers. The nest is unlined. The nesting season begins early in March. The female typically lays four to five white eggs, at two- to three-day intervals. She alone does the incubating, while the male feeds her at the nest. The female tends to sit tightly on the eggs if disturbed. Incubation lasts about three to four weeks. When the eggs hatch, the female continues to brood the nestlings for the first two weeks, while the male continues to bring food. The young begin to feed themselves and cast pellets at about ten days old. The nestlings leave the nest after five weeks. The adults may attack intruders at the nest or perform distraction displays.

Food: Western Screech Owls primarily eat small rodents, reptiles, and birds and large insects. They are strictly nocturnal hunters and begin hunting in open areas soon after dusk, staying near trees.

Will they use my yard? Western Screech Owls are more likely to be attracted to yards that provide a combination of large trees and open areas. They are more common along the Santa Ana River. If your yard is near the river, your chances of seeing, or hearing, a Western Screech Owl are better. Screech Owls are often associated with California Pepper Trees.

Western Screech Owls will use appropriately sized and properly located nest boxes. If you know you have Western Screech Owls in your neighborhood, consider placing such a nest box: it could be beneficial to the species, which has declined in numbers.

Key things to look for:
1) Smaller than a Robin. **2)** Ear tufts. **3)** Yellow eyes.

Northern Mockingbird   *Mimus polyglottos*

Spanish name: Cenzontle norteño

When can I expect to see them? Northern Mockingbirds are common year-round resident birds of southern California and native to the United States. They are one of the most widely known and popular songbirds in America.

What do they look like? Both sexes look alike. Mockingbirds are basically gray but have white wing patches that show when they fly. They are similar in size to Robins, but thinner.

Similar species: The only similar species occurring in the greater Inland Empire is the Loggerhead Shrike (not discussed); however, the Shrike is normally found in natural areas or at the extreme edges of urban areas only.

Behaviors: The Mockingbird is highly territorial, especially during breeding season, and will dive-bomb anything that comes close to its nest: pets, humans, and other birds.

Voice: The Mockingbird is known as the mimic of the bird world. Its scientific name even tells you this. Its genus name, *Mimus,* means "mimic," and its species name, *polyglottos,* means "many-tongued." The male incorporates the songs and calls of many other birds into its song and has been known to even include sounds like a telephone ringing or a train whistle. Unmated males will sing on moonlit nights during breeding season— *loudly,* to many people's dismay, for many hours. In the spring only the male sings, but in the fall the male and female sing.

Nesting: The nesting season begins as early as mid-February. The male and female build a cuplike nest in the crotch of tree branches or in a large shrub, usually within ten feet of the ground. The female lays three to five pale, blue-green, blotched eggs and does the incubating while the male stands guard. The eggs hatch in about two weeks and both parents tend the nestlings. Mockingbirds form long-term pair bonds and remain paired throughout the year. They will have two to three broods per year.

Food: Mockingbird food preferences vary by season. During the spring and summer they tend to eat insects. They run along, stop, and "wing-flash" to startle insects up from the ground. In the fall and winter they eat mainly fruits, especially those of pepper, fig, crabapple, and mulberry trees as well as pyracantha berries and grapes.

Will they use my yard? Mockingbirds especially like suburban yards that provide berries and other fruit, in addition to large shrubs and small trees for nesting. They will readily visit feeder tables but are pugnacious, so they may drive away other desirable species from your feeders.

Key things to look for:
1) Robin-sized. **2)** Gray and white. **3)** "Wing-flashes" as it looks for insects.

Northern Mockingbird wing-flashing

Northern Mockingbird adult

Rock Dove

Columba livia

Spanish name: Paloma doméstica

The Rock Dove is commonly known as a Pigeon.

When can I expect to see them? Rock Doves are year-round and common residents in the Inland Empire. Not native to California and the U.S., they were introduced to provide food. During World War I and World War II, the U.S. military used Rock Doves to move messages among the troops.

What do they look like? The Rock Dove is highly variable in color, from dark gray to white to multicolored. They usually have a white rump and a dark band on the end of the tail. The typical Rock Dove is blue-gray with iridescent feathers on the head and neck. Except that the male has a somewhat thicker neck than the female, both sexes look virtually alike. The Rock Dove has short, pink legs and feet and a small head.

Similar species: The Band-tailed Pigeon is a similar size (slightly larger) but always has a broad, pale gray band near the tip of the tail. It has a narrow white band on the nape of the neck, and it does not have a white rump.

Behaviors: The Rock Doves are gregarious. They feed, nest, and fly in groups.

Rock Doves are one of the swiftest birds in flight. When they take off quickly, their wings make a clapping or slapping noise that can sound like a car backfiring.

Voice: The male utters a frequent and sustained "cooing." Beginning birders can get a great example of courtship display behaviors by watching Rock Doves. The male struts before a female while bowing, tail-dragging, doing complete turns, and cooing. He may also do a wing-clapping display.

Nesting: The Rock Dove nest is a flimsy platform of sticks, twigs, and grasses. Nests are usually built under bridges, on rafters, on building ledges, or in palm trees. Rock Doves usually nest in colonies and have no real territories except for the immediate areas around their nests.

Rock Doves can breed in every month of the year and usually have several broods per year. The female lays one to two white eggs and incubates them for about two and a half weeks. The nestlings are fed on pigeon's

Rock Dove

Variations in Rock Dove color   Photo by Sylvia Gallagher

"milk," which is a special secretion from the crop of both sexes. It is extremely nutritious and contains more protein and fat than human or cow milk. The nestlings are exclusively fed on this "milk" for their first few days and continue to feed on it for over two weeks. The young first fly about a month after hatching.

Food: Rock Doves' heads bob as they walk along the ground in search of seed, grain, grasses, and clover. They will also eat some berries, bread crumbs, and table scraps.

Will they use my yard? The more urban the area, the better for Rock Doves, since they are very dependent on humans for food and shelter. Rock Doves can be seen in parks and fields around neighborhoods but are not common in more natural areas.

Key things to look for:
1) Dark band on the end of the tail. **2)** Pink feet. **3)** White rump (usually). **4)** A bit larger and heavier than a Robin. **5)** Often in a larger flock of similarly shaped birds with many color variations.

Band-Tailed Pigeon

Patagioenas fasciata

Spanish name: Paloma encinera

When can I expect to see them? Band-tailed Pigeons are native to the Pacific Coast states, but in the early 1900s they were almost hunted to extinction. They are now fairly common year-round residents of the Inland Empire. There are influxes of additional Band-tailed Pigeons during the winter from year to year as they wander in flocks, searching for food.

What do they look like? Band-tailed Pigeons are large birds with a typical pigeon shape but having a broad, pale gray band near the tip of the

Band-tailed Pigeon in flight

Band-tailed Pigeon

tail and a narrow white band on the nape of the neck. Their heads and chests are purplish. They have yellow bills tipped in black, and yellow legs. Males and females look alike and the male does not have a different breeding plumage.

Similar species: Band-tailed Pigeons are similar to Rock Doves (Pigeons) but larger. Flocks are uniform in color, rather than multicolored like the Rock Dove flocks. Band-tailed Pigeons have the pale gray tail band and no white on the rump.

Behaviors: Band-tailed Pigeons are swift, strong, and direct flyers, like the Rock Doves. They are gregarious and live in flocks that perch on the tops of trees. Often they go unnoticed, unless it is winter and the trees have lost their leaves.

Voice: The male frequently utters a deep, mellow call that is owl-like. It has two to three notes, the first slightly higher pitched than the others, sounding like "whoo-whoo."

Nesting: Band-tailed Pigeons begin nesting in early March and may have several broods per year. The female lays one white egg in the nest, and both sexes incubate the egg for about two and a half weeks. The nestling is fed on "pigeon's milk" (see Rock Dove description) and remains in the nest for about a month before it flies.

The nests are flimsy and shallow and made of sticks and twigs. Band-tailed Pigeons build their nests on branches of firs, oaks, and alders, usually near the trunk of the tree and within twenty feet of the ground.

Food: Their main food is nuts and berries, although they also consume insects in the summer. They are fond of acorns in the fall and winter.

Will they use my yard? The Band-tailed Pigeon most often frequents yards that have a mixture of large deciduous and evergreen trees and fruit-producing plants, such as toyon, elderberry, chokecherry, and coffeeberry. Band-tailed Pigeons can be lured into a yard by providing water and feeders with sunflower seeds, nuts, and berries, especially in the winter.

Key things to look for:
1) Large, heavy-set bird with small head. **2)** Broad, pale gray band on the tail near the tip. **3)** Yellow feet and bill. **4)** White band on nape of neck.

Cooper's Hawk

Accipiter cooperii

Spanish name: Gavilán de Cooper

When can I expect to see them? Cooper's Hawks are permanent residents and breeders of the Inland Empire. They can be seen at any time during the year, but their numbers increase in winter.

What do they look like? The Cooper's Hawk is about the size of a crow, 14 to 21 inches long, the male being smaller than the female. The adults look alike, with blue-gray upperparts and a white breast and belly cross-barred with red. The top of the head is blackish, and the tail is rounded and crossed with obscure blackish bars. The tail is relatively long, compared to the short, rounded wings. Cooper's Hawks, like other broad-winged hawks, have white undertail coverts that come up over the rump as they fly.

The immatures look like the adults but have brownish upperparts and white breasts and bellies streaked with brown.

Similar species: Study the **Look-alikes** pages. The Cooper's and the Sharp-shinned Hawk, similar in appearance, are both considered accipiters. Sharp-shinned Hawks are an uncommon winter visitor only. The best way to tell them apart is the overall shape when they soar. The Cooper's has a larger, more angular head that projects far beyond the wings when soaring. The Sharp-shinned's smaller head does not protrude beyond the wings.

Behaviors: Cooper's Hawks are often hard to see, since they perch quietly in the dense foliage of trees. The best time to see them is when they are flying. The flight pattern of the Cooper's Hawk is different from those of the high-flying Red-tailed and Red-shouldered Hawks. The Cooper's flies lower and circles rapidly, alternating between flapping and gliding, whereas the Red-tailed Hawk soars in great circles overhead and has slower wingbeats.

Cooper's Hawk in flight

Voice: Around the nest, they give a noisy alarm call sounding like "cack, cack, cack."

Nesting: The male selects the nest site, usually high in a conifer or a deciduous tree. The nest is built by both the male and female, of sticks and twigs, and is lined with chips and bark strips. The female usually adds her own feather down during and after laying. She lays four to five white eggs with a blue-green tint and brown spots. The female does most of the incubating, and the male does most of the hunting during incubation through the early nestling stage. Incubation takes about three weeks, and the young are in the nest for about a month before fledging. The adults continue to care for the young for thirty to forty days after they fledge.

Food: The Cooper's Hawk's favorite food is birds, especially Starlings, but also Robins, Mourning Doves, Flickers, Scrub Jays, and Woodpeckers. Hawks will take the young of other birds out of nests.

The Cooper's Hawk also eats small mammals, such as ground squirrels, and chickens and other farm poultry (Red-tailed Hawks usually get the blame, since they are more visible). It hunts by flying low and swift through brush and around trees, grabbing prey with talons while in the air or on the ground.

Will they use my yard? The Cooper's Hawk, although uncommon, is being found more regularly in suburban yards. It is a bird that most people do not want to attract, because the smaller birds using the bird feeders are its prey. If you have a feeder that is a magnet to small birds, you may very well have a Cooper's Hawk show up for dinner, too! It may be difficult to accept, but predation is part of nature. If a hawk becomes a common sight at your feeder, discourage it by abandoning the feeder and placing the birdseed under shrubs or in other, more protected, areas.

Key things to look for:
1) Crow-sized. **2)** Long, rounded tail. **3)** Short, broad wings.
4) White undertail coverts. **5)** Head extends beyond wings when flying.

Cooper's Hawk adult   *Cooper's Hawk immature*

BROWN: LIGHT TO DARK

House Wren

Troglodytes aedon

Spanish name: Saltapared-continental norteño

When can I expect to see them? House Wrens are year-round residents in southern California. They are migratory only in areas where winter temperatures normally drop below 40 degrees Fahrenheit, so they can be seen in the greater Inland Empire all year.

What do they look like? The House Wren is the plainest of all the wrens. It is 4½ to 5¼ inches long, unstreaked, gray-brown above and pale gray below, with a relatively short tail and a faint eyebrow. The wings and tail are finely barred.

Similar species: The Bewick's Wren is very similar in appearance to the House Wren at first glance, but the Bewick's has a distinct white eyebrow and a longer tail with white on it. There is a slight chance, if your house is close to an open, rocky area like Mt. Rubidoux or Box Springs, that you could also have a Rock Wren or even a Canyon Wren in your yard (neither one is described in this book, so check a field guide).

Behaviors: Like all wrens, the House Wren is fun to watch. Since the sexes look alike, watch for behavioral clues, especially during the breeding season, to see if you can tell them apart. For example, during courtship, the male sings while quivering his wings with his tail raised. The female responds by quivering her wings.

Voice: The male House Wren has a song of rich, descending warbles that lasts two to three seconds and is repeated many times, with a short pause in between. He sings from perches and throws his head back as he sings. The male and female have a harsh, buzzy scold note that they use as a warning of potential danger.

Nesting: House Wrens will nest in just about any crack or crevice, although they usually use a natural cavity or an old woodpecker hole. They've been known to nest in tin cans, old hats, old boots, and even in the axle of a car!

The male builds the foundation for one to seven nests, using sticks and twigs. The female looks them over and chooses which one she wants to use. She signals her interest to the male by bringing materials for the lining of the nest into the one she likes and finishing the nest building.

There are often six to eight eggs laid; they are white and heavily speckled with brown. The female incubates for about two weeks, and the male feeds her during this time. He also fiercely defends his territory during this time. The young leave the nest about two weeks after they are born. House Wrens may have two broods in a good year.

Food: House Wrens feed almost entirely on spiders and insects: stinkbugs, leafhoppers, grasshoppers, caterpillars, and beetles.

House Wren

Will they use my yard? House Wrens will use any suburban yard, and urban settings of higher density. They prefer areas of dense vegetation. They will use properly designed nest boxes or anything else suitable for nesting. A friend of mine recently had a pair nesting in her barbecue grill!

Key things to look for:
1) Cocked tail. **2)** Small, active bird. **3)** No distinct white eyebrow. **4)** Faint barring on wings and tail. **5)** Usually found in dense vegetation.

House Wren nests on an automobile engine

Bewick's Wren

Thryomanes bewickii

Spanish name: Saltapared de Bewick

When can I see them? Bewick's Wrens are permanent, year-round residents of the Inland Empire. They are very sedentary, with little seasonal movement, sticking closely to year-round territories.

What do they look like? Bewick's Wrens are chunky and small, only 5¼ inches in length. The male and female look the same, with dark brown-gray unstreaked backs and long, white eye stripes. The long, rounded tails are edged with white spots and are usually cocked upwards. The bills are slender and slightly down-curved.

Similar species: The House Wren is a similar size and shape, but with a plain brown color and only a faint eye stripe; its wings and tail are finely barred. The Bewick's Wren may also be confused with a female sparrow.

Behaviors: Bewick's Wrens are quick, active birds that have the habit of flicking their tails sideways. When singing, the male holds his head high and tucks his tail down and under. Wrens are highly inquisitive and can often be lured into view with squeaky noises.

Voice: Both sexes sing a loud trilling song that is variable but consists of a high, thin buzz and a warble. Like all wrens, they have a scolding "buzz" call that they use frequently, especially when they perceive danger near their nests or young.

Nesting: Bewick's Wrens nest in natural cavities almost anywhere, in trees, fence posts, old woodpecker holes, mailboxes, and even tin cans and baskets. The nest materials are primarily green mosses, sticks, and dead leaves, and nests are lined with feathers. The female usually lays five to seven (sometimes as many as eleven) spotted eggs that she alone incubates. The eggs hatch in about two weeks, at which time she and the male feed the young. The young fledge about two weeks later. Bewick's Wrens will have two to three broods per year.

Food: Bewick's Wrens eat virtually nothing but insects. They forage on the ground, in shrubs, and along the limbs of trees. They are constantly flitting in and out of every hole and crevice. In the morning I have

Bewick's Wren   Photo by Charles Melton

watched them go in and out of the hanging plants and baskets on my patio looking for insects.

Will they use my yard? The Bewick's Wren likes to use suburban yards, close to houses, especially if there are adequate shrubs and trees with potential nesting cavities. They also will use nest boxes if you provide them.

Key things to look for:
1) Small, dark brown-gray bird. **2)** White eye stripe. **3)** Flicks tail.
4) White edges on tail near tip.

House Sparrow

Passer domesticus

Spanish name: Gorrión doméstico

The House Sparrow is also commonly referred to as the English Sparrow.

When can I expect to see them? The House Sparrow is not a native. It was introduced into New York City from Europe in the mid-1800s to control insects. It quickly spread westward and is now extremely abundant in most parts of the Inland Empire throughout the year.

What do they look like? The House Sparrow is your "typical" sparrow, about 5¼ to 6¼ inches long, dingy brown, with a large head and heavy, conical bill. The male can be seen in breeding and nonbreeding plumage, depending on the time of year. In breeding plumage, the male has a gray crown, black bib, black bill, and chestnut on the nape of the neck. In nonbreeding plumage, he has a grayer appearance, with less distinct markings. His bill changes from black to brownish.

The female is brown overall, darker and streaked on the back, with a lighter, unstreaked breast and belly. She has a broad, buff-colored eye stripe.

Similar species: The female House Sparrow could be confused with a female House Finch, except she has an unstreaked breast (the House Finch has heavy streaking on the breast). In the winter, the female could also be confused with a female Chipping Sparrow (much less common), and with the immature White-crowned Sparrow (much less common). See **Look-alikes** pages for comparisons.

Of the sparrows that occur in the Inland Empire, the male could possibly be confused with a Song Sparrow or a Dark-eyed Junco. The Song Sparrow has a central, dark breast spot rather than a black bib. The Junco has an all-black head, not just a black bib.

Behaviors: House Sparrows are boisterous and often aggressive toward other birds. They often form large, noisy flocks and roost in city trees.

Like the Starling, the House Sparrow does not have a prenuptial molt, but acquires its breeding plumage by wearing down the gray breast feathers, leaving a black bib.

Voice: The House Sparrow's call is one of the most common noises of a city, a constant "cheep, cheep, cheep." Although it is considered a song-bird, the male certainly has no real musical song.

Nesting: House Sparrows are aggressive and prolific nesters. They will use just about any place to build a nest: a bird box, a natural tree hollow, eaves, rafters, palms, and cypress branches. They have been known to chase less aggressive birds away from nest sites.

They will raise two to three broods a year, and they will start copulating again even when they have nestlings still in the nest. House Sparrows have been reported to nest throughout the year, although most frequently from April to September. Both sexes build the nest, usually of grasses and forbs. The nest is lined with a lot of feathers. The female lays five eggs that are white, pale blue, or green, and marked with darker blotches. She does most of the incubating, for about two weeks. The young are fed regurgitated insects by both parents and leave the nest about two weeks after being hatched.

Food: The House Sparrow is one of the most resourceful birds in the city. It can be seen picking bugs off the grills of cars and drinking water from swamp coolers! It feeds on nearly anything that can be found in a city: insects, weeds, fruit, and garbage.

Will they use my yard? House Sparrows will use just about any yard in the Inland Empire, from very urban to suburban, actually preferring the more urban! You probably won't have to attract these birds; they'll most likely

House Sparrow female

be in your yard no matter what you do. They are attracted to seed put out in feeders. To discourage them, do not provide cracked corn, one of their favorites.

Key things to look for:
1) Typical sparrow shape and size. **2)** In large, noisy flocks. **3)** Unstreaked breast.

House Sparrow male in nonbreeding plumage

House Sparrow male in breeding plumage

Song Sparrow
Melospiza melodia

Spanish name: Gorrión cantor

When can I expect to see them? Song Sparrows are permanent, year-round residents of the Inland Empire, although their numbers appear to be declining.

What do they look like? The Song Sparrow is a medium-sized bird with a typical sparrow look. It has a dark brown head, back, and tail with a lighter, heavily streaked breast and a breast spot. Young birds have finer streaks and may not have a central breast spot.

Similar species: The Song Sparrow could be confused with other sparrow or finch females that have streaked breasts. The distinguishing feature is the central breast spot.

Behaviors: When they are flushed, Song Sparrows typically pump their tails as they fly low, looking for cover.

Voice: In contrast to its somewhat drab appearance, the Song Sparrow has a melodious voice. The song begins with one to three distinct notes that then run into a buzzy trill that often slows at the end.

Song Sparrow

Nesting: The nest can be on the ground, under grasses, brush piles, or bushes, or low in a small tree or shrub. The female builds the nest and lays three to four blue-green eggs, which are heavily spotted. The female incubates for about two weeks. The male and female tend the young, which fledge in less than two weeks. They may have two broods per year.

Song Sparrows are one of the most frequent Cowbird "hosts," which may account for why they are less common now than they have been historically in the Inland Empire.

Food: The Song Sparrow primarily eats insects but will also eat grass seed and some berries.

Will they use my yard? Song Sparrows prefer thick underbrush in riparian areas. They can also be seen in suburban yards, especially those with thick shrubbery, thick tangles of berry-producing plants, and brush piles. Song Sparrows will feed at ground feeders if offered birdseed. They are also attracted to water.

Key things to look for:
1) Dark brown upperparts. **2)** Heavily streaked breast. **3)** Central breast spot.

Cedar Waxwing

Bombycilla cedrorum

Spanish name: Ampelis Americano

When can I expect to see them? Cedar Waxwings are only fall and winter visitors to the Inland Empire, arriving usually around September and gone by May. They breed farther north.

What do they look like? Cedar Waxwings are beautiful birds, with their crested heads, black masks, soft brown, silky-looking feathers, and yellow-tipped tails. They have yellow bellies. Adult birds often have red, waxy tips on the wing feathers.

Juveniles are light brown-gray and have streaked underparts. They lack the red, waxy wing tips and have little or no black around the eye or throat.

Similar species: There is no other bird in the Inland Empire that could be confused with the Cedar Waxwing, if you get a good look at it. If the lighting is poor and you only have a silhouette, the shape and crest could look like a Phainopepla. However, Phainopeplas do not move in flocks and are not commonly seen in the winter.

Behaviors: Cedar Waxwings occur in flocks of about ten to twenty during their stay in the Inland Empire. They can be seen flying "as one" into

Cedar Waxwing

the treetops, then descending, still a single unit, to your yard or birdbath. They maintain a constant calling to each other as they do this.

Voice: Their call is a very high, thin, soft, one-note whistle or series of "zeees."

Nesting: Cedar Waxwings do not nest in the Inland Empire. They nest primarily in Canada and Alaska in coniferous and birch forests.

Food: The main diet of the Cedar Waxwing consists of berries from such plants as cotoneaster, elderberry, pyracantha, cedar, and privet, and fleshy fruit, such as apples and crabapples.

Will they use my yard? Cedar Waxwings are attracted to suburban yards, especially if the trees and shrubs provide berries and other fruit. Waxwings will come to feeding tables with cut-up fruit, especially apples and raisins. They are also attracted to birdbaths, for drinking and bathing.

Key things to look for:
1) Brownish bird. **2)** Crested head. **3)** Red, waxy "droplets" on the wing tips. **4)** Yellow-tipped tail. **5)** Flocks move "as one." **6)** High, thin, soft "whistle."

Cedar Waxwing

California Towhee

Pipilo crissalis

Spanish name: Rascador Californiano

Until recently, the California Towhee was called the Brown Towhee.

When can I expect to see them? The California Towhee is a highly sedentary, year-round resident of the Inland Empire.

What do they look like? The California Towhee is an inconspicuous, drab brown bird the size of a Robin (8½ to 10 inches), with a fairly long tail. Males and females look alike. The California Towhee's head, back, and tail are dark brown and the underparts are a lighter brown. It has rusty undertail coverts and a buff-colored throat bordered by a broken black "necklace." Its bill is short and conical. It has yellowish legs. The juveniles have streaked underparts.

Similar species: The California Towhee could be confused with several birds that you may see in your yard, including the female Brewer's Blackbird, the female Brown-headed Cowbird, and the female House Finch (see **Look-alikes** pages). These species, however, are smaller and tend to form flocks, unlike the Towhee.

Behaviors: California Towhees are strongly territorial during breeding season and aggressively defend their territories. I've watched a Towhee fight his image in my car's side mirror for minutes on end, as if his reflection were another male.

The California Towhee is not a strong flier and utilizes its legs for locomotion.

Voice: The male and female California Towhees make a strong, metallic "chink" call. The male runs these together and calls it a song! The Towhee pair has an elongated "contact squeal" that they emit upon reuniting in a bush, as a means of maintaining their lifelong bond.

Nesting: California Towhees usually build their bulky nests three to twelve feet from the ground in shrubs and trees. Their breeding season begins in early March. They are attracted to dense tangles of vines and shrubs for nesting. The female usually lays three eggs in a deep cup made of small twigs, weeds, and grass. The eggs are pale blue-green and are marked with various brown blotches. The female is the only one to incubate, but after the nestlings are born, the male and female both feed them insects. The young leave the nest in about eight days.

The pair will nest one or two more times in a season. The young of the first nest remain with the adults until the next brood hatches, at which time they are driven away by the parents.

The California Towhee's nest is often parasitized by the Brown-headed Cowbird. The female Cowbird lays her eggs in the nest, leaving them to be raised by the Towhees.

Food: California Towhees feed primarily on insects and seeds by scratching around in leaf litter and under brush. They may also eat garden seedlings!

Will they use my yard? California Towhees will use yards that provide them with dense vegetation for nesting and foraging. Since they like to feed in leaf litter, do not rake your leaves from under your shrubs if you hope to attract them! Provide them with birdseed, bread, and grain at low-to-the-ground feeding stations.

Key things to look for:
1) Brown all over. **2)** Rust under the long tail. **3)** Feeds on the ground.
4) Makes "chink, chink, chink" sound.

California Towhee

Hermit Thrush

Catharus guttatus

Spanish name: Zorzalito colirrufo

When can I expect to see them? Hermit Thrushes are uncommon winter visitors to the Inland Empire, arriving in October and leaving by the end of March. Due to their secretive ways, they are not often noticed. They are more noticeable during migration, since they occur then in larger numbers.

What do they look like? The Hermit Thrush is a Robin-sized brown bird with a spotted breast, a conspicuous white eye ring, and a reddish tail. Both sexes look alike.

Similar species: The Hermit Thrush is easily confused with the Swainson's Thrush (not discussed), an uncommon spring migrant that arrives only after the Hermit Thrush is gone. The California Towhee may be confused with the Hermit Thrush if seen from the back.

Behaviors: Hermit Thrushes are regular visitors but rather shy, so they may go unnoticed. They habitually flick their wings.

Voice: In the winter, the rapid "chup-chup" call can be heard. The male Hermit Thrush has a beautiful song, but unfortunately, we don't hear it often in Riverside.

Hermit Thrush

Nesting: The Hermit Thrush nests from our western mountains all the way up to northern Canada, preferring coniferous and mixed woodland forests.

Food: Hermit Thrushes are insect eaters primarily, although they will also eat berries, especially of the toyon shrub, in the winter. They search for insects in leafy litter and will run along the ground while foraging.

Will they use my yard? Hermit Thrushes are attracted to berry-producing shrubs and trees in suburban yards in the wintertime. They will visit back-yard feeders if fruit is provided. Dripping water will also attract them.

Key things to look for:
1) Brownish bird. **2)** Spotted breast. **3)** Reddish brown tail. **4)** White eye ring. **5)** Shy. **6)** Flicks wings.

Killdeer

Charadrius vociferus

Spanish name: Chorlito tildío

When can I expect to see them? Killdeer are fairly common permanent residents and breeders of the Inland Empire. Their numbers increase in the wintertime, when they can be seen in small flocks.

What do they look like? Killdeer are actually shorebirds, even though they are often found far from water. They are Robin-sized with fairly long legs. Both sexes are similar, with two black chest bands. They have brown backs and rusty rumps.

Similar species: There are no similar-looking species that occur in yards of the Inland Empire.

Behaviors: The Killdeer is best known for its distraction display, often referred to as a broken-wing display; the adult looks as if it has an injured wing as it lures the potential predator (often a human) away from the nest. Once the predator is far enough away, the adult Killdeer flies off.

Voice: The Killdeer got its name because of its alarm call, which sounds just like its name: "killdeer-killdeer," given in a fairly loud, insistent voice.

Nesting: The Killdeer usually nests in a depression on the ground in the open, so that it has good views all around it. The "nest" is located in areas that have camouflaging stones or gravel nearby to conceal both the eggs and the young.

The female typically lays four blotched, buff eggs. The male and female both incubate, for about a month. The young are born precocial: able to leave the nest within an hour of hatching! They then "follow" the parents and begin feeding on their own. I put "follow" in quotation marks because I have watched the adults rushing around, apparently trying to keep up with the young, who are running every which way. During this time, the young are incredibly well camouflaged, nearly indistinguishable from their surroundings. They are able to fly in about three weeks.

Food: The majority of the food eaten by Killdeer is insects, with the remainder being worms and grubs.

Will they use my yard? Killdeer prefer large, open fields or expansive lawns for feeding, and sandy, gravelly areas (including new housing developments) for nesting. So if you are building a house in the springtime, keep an eye out for the very camouflaged nest and young.

Key things to look for:

1) Robin-sized. **2)** Two black breast bands. **3)** Long legs. **4)** Ground dwellers in open areas.

Killdeer distraction display
Photo by Warren Lemey

Killdeer chick   Photo by Sylvia Gallagher

Killdeer adult

Mourning Dove   *Zenaida macroura*

Spanish name: Paloma huilota

The Mourning Dove is often referred to as the Turtle Dove.

When can I expect to see them? Mourning Doves can be seen all year, as they are common, permanent residents and breeders of the Inland Empire.

What do they look like? The Mourning Dove is a sleek-bodied bird, slightly larger than a Scrub Jay, with gray-brown plumage above and a peachy wash underneath. For the most part, the male and female look alike, although the female is slightly smaller and duller in color. The Mourning Dove has a long, tapered tail, orange feet, and a dark bill. The white tips on the outer tail feathers can be seen when it flies. The male does not have a different breeding plumage. Juveniles have heavy spotting on their breasts and their wings have a scaled appearance.

Similar species: The Mourning Dove is slimmer than either the Rock Dove (Pigeon) or the Band-tailed Pigeon, neither of which has the long, tapered tail of the Mourning Dove. The Spotted Dove (not discussed), which is now rare in the Inland Empire, is the most similar in size and shape, but it has a spotted collar that may be obscure in young birds.

Behaviors: The Mourning Dove has strong, swift flight, and its wings produce a loud, fluttering whistle as it flies. It is easiest to see Mourning Doves when they are flying or perched on telephone wires. They are quiet and often go unnoticed. When Mourning Doves are not breeding, they live in loose flocks.

Unlike other birds, Pigeons and Doves can drink water like horses do, by immersing their bills and sucking up the water.

Voice: The common name of the Mourning Dove comes from the "mournful," low-pitched cooing that the male "sings" from prominent perches to defend its territory. The female gives a softer version of the male's song.

Nesting: Mourning Doves mate for life. The nests are very flimsy, built of a few crossed sticks and twigs. The male brings the female twigs, and she places and arranges them, usually in the crotch of a tree. Mourning Doves have been known, however, to nest just about anywhere: on the ground, on the tops of rocks, in vines, in roof gutters, etc.

Mourning Doves will nest during any month of the year in southern California. The female usually lays two white eggs. For about two weeks, both adults incubate the eggs; the male in the day, and the female at night. The young leave the nest after about two weeks and are on their own within a week of that. Because of our climate in southern California, Mourning Doves produce two to five broods a year.

Like all members of the Pigeon family, the nestlings are fed for the first few days on a substance called pigeon's milk that has a high fat content and apparently has a growth-producing vitamin. Both the male and female regurgitate this liquid, and the nestlings stick their bills into the throats of the adults to drink. After about five days, the young are fed grain.

Food: Mourning Doves feed almost exclusively on seeds. They eat tremendous amounts of weed seeds, in addition to such things as waste grain, peanuts, and pine seeds. They swallow gravel and retain it in their gizzards (stomachs) to help grind the seeds, as do most seed-eating birds. They walk along the ground with their tiny heads bobbing up and down as they feed.

Mourning Dove

Will they use my yard? Mourning Doves are found throughout the Inland Empire in all types of residential areas. They are abundant and widespread, so there is a strong possibility that they will use your yard. Mourning Doves are easily attracted to yards that provide seed directly on the ground or at low feeding platforms. They don't eat from hanging feeders. They also are attracted to water.

Key things to look for:
1) Pale brown bird. **2)** Long, tapered tail. **3)** Small, bobbing head. **4)** Cooing sound. **5)** Wings whistle when they take off in flight.

Barn Owl   *Tyto alba*

Spanish name: Lechuza de campanario

When can I expect to see them? Barn Owls are common year-round residents of the Inland Empire. They often go unnoticed, since they are nocturnal. They roost in dense trees during the day.

What do they look like? Barn Owls are large and pale, with dark eyes in a heart-shaped, monkey-like face. They have no ear tufts. They have long, feathered legs and large feet with sharp talons. Both sexes look alike, although the female is slightly larger.

Similar species: The Great Horned Owl is larger and darker than the Barn Owl and has ear tufts. The Western Screech Owl is smaller and darker and has ear tufts.

Behaviors: As the name "Barn Owl" suggests, this is a species that will use barns and abandoned buildings. Thus it is the owl most closely associated with humans. Like all owls, Barn Owls regurgitate pellets of indigestible fur and bone. When perched, they have the habit of lowering their heads and swaying them from side to side.

Barn Owl   Photo by Peter Bloom

Voice: The call of the Barn Owl is a raspy, hissing screech. Barn Owls also have a call that is a long, drawn-out clicking.

Nesting: Barn Owls do not build an actual nest; they nest in hollow tree cavities or in buildings and are commonly found nesting in the Inland Empire. Barn Owls mate for life. The female lays five to seven white eggs, laid at two- to three-day intervals. The female incubates for about a month, and the male feeds her during this time. Because the eggs are laid at intervals, the first owlet may be several weeks old when the last egg hatches.

The nestlings are tended and fed by both parents, and they become feathered between the third and seventh week. They fly at about sixty days old and are independent about three weeks after that.

Food: Barn Owls hunt for rodents, primarily. They swoop low over the ground in search of prey, which often makes them vulnerable to cars when they pass over roadways. They hunt by sound as well as by sight. Their feathers are soft, allowing them to fly silently in search of prey. Barn Owls are actually able to hear the sound of a mouse's heart beating under three feet of snow!

Will they use my yard? Barn Owls are known to roost in palm trees with thick thatches, so if you have palms in your yard, you may have them. Barn Owls will even nest in constructed nest boxes.

Key things to look for:
1) Large, pale owl. 2) Heart-shaped face.

Great Horned Owl

Bubo virginianus

Spanish name: Buho cornudo

When can I expect to see them? Great Horned Owls are very sedentary, permanent residents and breeders of the Inland Empire.

What do they look like? The Great Horned Owl is the largest of the North American "eared" owls, being 18 to 25 inches long. The female is much larger than the male and can attain a wingspan of 5 feet. The "horns" are actually tufts of feathers; the ears are lower down the sides of the head.

The Great Horned Owl has a bulky brown body spotted with darker brown, and it has white throat feathers. It uses its massive talons to catch prey.

Like all owls, the Great Horned Owl has fluffy wing feathers that make its flight almost soundless, a great advantage when hunting.

Similar species: There is no other owl found in the Inland Empire that is as large as the Great Horned Owl.

Behaviors: The Great Horned, like all owls, regurgitates pellets of indigestible animal parts, such as bone and fur. It often drops the pellets below its roost or nest.

Also like all owls, Great Horned Owls have immobile eyes, so that they have to turn their heads to look at something. Some people think that owls can turn their heads 360 degrees, but this is not true.

Voice: The typical call is a deep, soft, resonating series of three to eight hoots: "whoo-whoo, whoo-whoo," just like you hear in scary movie sound effects. A lot of hooting goes on during courtship. The Great Horned Owl also has a bark call, and the young make an eerie scream when hungrily pursuing the parents.

Nesting: Great Horned Owls are early nesters, starting as early as January. They often take over nests of hawks and crows, and they have been known to nest in large palms and tall eucalyptus trees, as well as in tree cavities. Although a pair may occupy a territory for years, they may not nest in the same site every year.

The female lays two or three large white eggs. Both the male and female incubate the eggs for approximately a month. The young don't leave the nest for two to two and a half months, and the adults fiercely defend the young during this time. The adults continue to feed the fledglings for weeks, until the young learn to hunt on their own.

Food: Great Horned Owls will eat anything they can catch, although their favorite foods are jackrabbits and cottontails. They will eat skunk and other mammals (yes, even including a cat or two) and occasionally large birds, like ducks and geese. Like all owls, Great Horned Owls use their acute hearing and big, bright yellow eyes to detect the slightest movement and can therefore hunt very effectively at low light levels.

Will they use my yard? Great Horned Owls are a lot more common than you would think, even in residential neighborhoods. Since they are nocturnal, they are rarely seen but frequently heard. This is another bird that you probably wouldn't try to attract to your yard. However, if you have palm trees or tall trees, like eucalyptus, a Great Horned Owl may be there. Look for pellets.

Key things to look for:
1) Large owl. **2)** Ear tufts. **3)** Makes "whoo-whoo" sounds.

Great Horned Owl adult

Great Horned Owl adult with nestlings
Photo by Russell Kerr

Greater Roadrunner

Geococcyx californianus

Spanish name: Correcaminos mayor

When can I expect to see them? Greater Roadrunners are year-round residents and breeders of the Inland Empire, so they may be seen at any time.

What do they look like? The Roadrunner is a large, upright bird with a crested head and long tail. The breast and upperparts are brown and streaked. Iridescence in the tail and upperparts is visible only at close range. There is a patch of blue and red behind the eye. The immatures lack the eye patch. The sexes look alike.

Similar species: There is no other bird in the Inland Empire that could be confused with the unique Roadrunner.

Behaviors: Roadrunners are weak flyers and move primarily by running swiftly along the ground or up into trees to escape predators and catch prey. They like to sun themselves and actually have dark, featherless patches on their sides to help them warm up. They take dust baths and practice anting.

Voice: No, they do not go "beep-beep" as the Roadrunner in the cartoon does. The male has a long, descending "oo-oo-oo" song that he makes

Greater Roadrunner

from the top of a large rock or the branches of a dead tree, usually at dawn. It's funny to see a Roadrunner "sing," since its head descends along with the sound! The Roadrunner also has a variety of clucks and whines and clacks its bill in rapid succession.

Nesting: Although the Roadrunner is a member of the Cuckoo family, whose members are known for laying their eggs in the nests of others, the Roadrunner does not do this. It builds its own nest and raises its own young.

The Roadrunner builds a large stick nest, usually three to fifteen feet above the ground in a shrub. The female lays four to six white eggs the size of chicken eggs. The male does most of the incubation, especially at night. They perform distraction displays to protect the nest. The pair bond is permanent, as is the territory. The eggs hatch after three weeks, and the young are tended by both parents. The young leave the nest in three weeks, at which time they are able to catch their own food.

Food: Roadrunners are meat eaters, preferring lizards, snakes, large insects, and small birds. They've been known to pick off hummingbirds at feeders! They will eat some berries also.

Will they use my yard? If you live near a large, open, grassy or natural area, you are likely to have a Roadrunner visit your yard at some point in time. They may come in search of lizards and large insects.

Friends of mine had a pair of Roadrunners that nested in their carport, on top of kayaks!

Key things to look for:
1) Very large. **2)** Brown. **3)** Bushy crest. **4)** Long tail. **5)** Runs along ground swiftly, only flying in short spurts.

MULTICOLORED:
THREE DISTINCT COLORS

Cliff Swallow

Petrochelidon pyrrhonota

Spanish name: Golondrina risquera

When can I expect to see them? Cliff Swallows are spring and summer residents and breeders of the Inland Empire. They arrive from mid-February through early March and depart early in the fall for their winter homes in South America. During migration, they may be joined by large numbers of other swallow species, such as the Violet-Green Swallow, the Northern Rough-winged Swallow, and the Tree Swallow. Look for these large groups overhead—unlike most birds, they migrate during the day. This allows them to continue to catch the insects they feed upon.

What do they look like? Cliff Swallows are small, 5 to 6 inches long, with long, pointed wings and slender bodies. The sexes are similar, with cream-colored foreheads, dark throats, and glossy blue-black wings, tails, and backs. The back has small white striping. Unlike other swallows in the area, Cliff Swallows have rusty rumps and square tails. Immatures are similar to the adults, but duller. They retain this plumage until the fall migration.

Similar species: Although there are several other species of swallows in the Inland Empire, most will probably not use your yard, other than to fly over it catching insects.

Behaviors: This is the swallow of San Juan Capistrano fame. Legend has it that they return on the same day every year, and they do, give or take several days—which is pretty amazing, since they migrate from South America!

Like all swallows, Cliff Swallows are very active and adept flyers. They have tiny feet, since most of their activity takes place on the wing. They can be seen perched, however, in long rows on rooftops and telephone wires.

Voice: The Cliff Swallow keeps up a continual chatter and twitter as it flies to and from the nest. The "song" is not musical; it is composed of squeaking, creaking notes.

Nesting: Cliff Swallows build gourd-shaped mud nests with a narrow, sometimes protruding entrance on the side. In about one

Cliff Swallow

week, a pair will build a nest from mud they carry in their mouths. Cliff Swallows like to nest in colonies with sometimes as many as a thousand nests. They colonize in locations where the nests can be packed together along a vertical surface, such as under a bridge. The nests are often repaired and reused. However, House Sparrows are more aggressive than Cliff Swallows and will sometimes take over their nests. This may account for local fluctuations in Cliff Swallow numbers.

The female Cliff Swallow lays four to five whitish eggs, sometimes dotted with brown. Both parents incubate the eggs for about two weeks. Cliff Swallows nesting in dense colonies sometimes parasitize the nests of other Cliff Swallows. A female will lay eggs quickly while another female is out of her nest. The young, including the "adopted" nestlings, are tended by both the male and female and leave the nest in about two weeks.

Food: Cliff Swallows eat insects, including mosquitoes, catching them on the wing. Their short bills and wide mouths are ideal for this.

Will they use my yard? Cliff Swallows have readily adapted to built structures and are becoming increasingly common. People either love them or hate them. Cliff Swallows like to build their nests under eaves (especially in new housing developments). If swallows nest near you, I encourage you to leave the nests alone and allow your family to experience these birds as they raise their own families. They *do* create a mess, but hosing down the walkways can easily take care of this. If these birds choose to spend a month raising their young at *your* house, I hope you will feel honored.

Key things to look for:
1) Swift, adept flyer. **2)** Square tail. **3)** Rusty rump. **4)** Cream-colored forehead.

Cliff Swallow adult collecting mud for nest   *Cliff Swallow nest colony*

Dark-Eyed Junco

Junco hyemalis

Spanish name: Junco ojioscuro

They are also referred to as Oregon Juncos.

When can I expect to see them? In the Inland Empire, Dark-eyed Juncos are common winter visitors between October and April.

What do they look like? Juncos are small, attractive birds, about the size and shape of sparrows. They have blackish heads and chests that contrast sharply with their white bellies. Their backs are reddish brown, and their sides are buff-orange. They have white outer tail feathers. The female is slightly drabber than the male.

Similar species: The Dark-eyed Junco could be confused with the resident Spotted Towhee, which is larger, has rows of white spots on the wings, and has red eyes. The Black Phoebe also has a blackish head, but the black extends farther down onto the sides, back, and wings on the Phoebe.

Behaviors: Juncos can be seen in loose flocks in the winter. They are fairly nervous little birds and will fly to cover, twittering, with the slightest sign of danger.

Dark-eyed Junco male

Voice: The male's song is a series of trills, all at the same pitch, sounding like a sewing machine needle going up and down. The male and female both have a rapid twittering call and a sharp "dit" that they give when feeding and when flushed off the ground into a nearby bush or tree.

Nesting: Juncos do not breed in the Inland Empire; they choose nesting sites in fairly dense evergreen forests, including areas in the San Bernardino and San Jacinto Mountains.

Food: Juncos are seedeaters and feed on the ground.

Will they use my yard? Juncos will use suburban yards, especially those with parklike settings—open areas interspersed with trees and shrubs. Juncos will come to backyard bird feeders if the feeding platform is close to the ground. They are attracted to seeds of annuals and perennials in gardens and to yards with evergreen trees, where they roost.

Key things to look for:
1) Sparrow shape and size. **2)** Blackish head, chestnut brown back, and white belly. **3)** White outer tail feathers.

Dark-eyed Junco female

Western Tanager

Piranga ludoviciana

Spanish name: Tangara occidental

When can I expect to see them? Western Tanagers are spring and fall migrants through the Inland Empire, traveling to either their breeding grounds in more northern forests or their wintering grounds in Central America.

What do they look like? The male Western Tanager is a beautifully colored bird when in breeding plumage, with a reddish orange head, yellow body, and black wings and tail. The nonbreeding plumage of the male is similar to the female's olive-yellow overall, because he loses most of the red on his head. The Western Tanager is smaller than a Robin and has a fairly stout bill. There are two conspicuous wing bars, the upper being yellow and the lower being yellowish or white.

Similar species: The female's coloration and the nonbreeding plumage of the male could be confused with the female Oriole's. However, Orioles have thinner bills and appear in this area at different times of the year.

Behaviors: In spite of the male's coloration, it is difficult to see this bird: amazingly enough, it blends well with tree foliage. The easiest way to find the Western Tanager is to learn its song and call.

Western Tanager female

Voice: Western Tanagers have a "brtt" call. The male's song is a loud series of two- to three-syllable notes separated by pauses.

Nesting: Western Tanagers nest in coniferous forests, mostly in the mountains; some nest as far north as Alaska.

Food: The Tanagers are primarily insect eaters, but they will also eat some fruit.

Will they use my yard? Western Tanagers may stop to use your suburban yard as they are migrating. Tanagers have been known to use fruiting mulberry and alder trees, so keep your eyes open if you have these trees.

Key things to look for:
1) Two distinct wing bars. **2)** Male: red, yellow, and black plumage.
3) Female: olive-yellow with dull olive to gray back and wings.

Western Tanager male in breeding plumage

Western Tanager male in nonbreeding plumage

Spotted Towhee

Pipilo maculatus

Spanish name: Rascador ojirrojo

In older bird books, the Spotted Towhee is referred to as the Rufous-sided Towhee.

When can I expect to see them? Spotted Towhees are uncommon year-round residents and breeders of the Inland Empire.

What do they look like? The Spotted Towhee is medium-sized, several inches smaller than a Robin. The male has a black hood and upperparts, chestnut sides, and white underparts. The female has a similar pattern, except the head, breast, and upperparts are browner than the male's. Both the male and female have two white wing bars, in addition to white spots on the wings and white corners on the tail that can be seen when they fly. They have long tails and red eyes. Juveniles have the same wing pattern as adults. Juveniles look similar to females, except they have streaking on their breasts.

Similar species: The Spotted Towhee male is similar to the Robin, but the Robin has no white on the breast, wings, or tail. The Dark-eyed Junco

Spotted Towhee

is smaller and only occurs in the fall and winter. The Spotted Towhee male could also be confused with a Black-headed Grosbeak male, which has an orange breast and a shorter tail, and which primarily occurs as a migrant.

At first glance, the female Spotted Towhee could be confused with the California Towhee. The California Towhee, however, does not have any white on its wings or tail.

Behaviors: Spotted Towhees are shy birds. They are easier to hear than see; they can be heard rustling around in dead leaves. However, they are curious, like many other birds, and will come out to investigate if you make squeaky noises on the back of your hand.

Voice: The male's song varies, but the calls include a whining "chee-ee" that goes up in pitch at the end and a raspy "mew."

Nesting: Spotted Towhees usually nest on the ground or in dense underbrush or shrubs within five feet of the ground. The female builds a well-concealed yet bulky nest of leaves, strips of bark, weed stalks, grasses, and twigs. She lines it with grasses and other softer materials. She lays three to four eggs that are creamy or grayish in color with reddish brown spots. She alone incubates the eggs, for about two weeks. At first, both parents feed the young by regurgitation. The young leave the nest in about eight to ten days. Spotted Towhees will often raise two broods per year.

Spotted Towhees' nests have been parasitized by Brown-headed Cowbirds.

Food: The Towhees feed on insects, seeds, and berries found on the ground. They use their feet as rakes, scratching and kicking both feet backwards at the same time. Often you cannot see them but will hear them scratching.

Will they use my yard? Spotted Towhees occur in suburban yards only if the shrubbery is dense enough and the yards are not too well manicured. Towhees like leaf litter left under the shrubs. They are attracted to birdseed and suet provided at a ground feeder set close to shrubs. They are also attracted to water.

Key things to look for:
1) Black, white, and chestnut. **2)** White wing bars. **3)** Spots on the tail. **4)** White corners on the long tail, visible when it flies. **5)** Feeds mostly on the ground and scratches backwards with its feet.

American Kestrel
Falco sparverius

Spanish name: Cernícalo Americano

Often referred to as a Sparrow Hawk.

When can I expect to see them? The American Kestrel is a year-round resident and breeder of the Inland Empire.

What do they look like? The Kestrel is the smallest falcon in our area, about Robin size (10½ inches). As is typical of falcons, the Kestrel has long, narrow, pointed wings and a longish tail. Both males and females have rust-colored backs and tails and two black stripes on a white face. The sexes can be distinguished by wing color; the male has blue-gray wings, and the female has rust brown wings.

Similar species: The only other falcon occurring in the Inland Empire, but less likely to be seen in your yard, is the Merlin. The Merlin is larger and lacks the strong facial markings of the Kestrel. In addition, the Merlin is only a winter visitor.

Behaviors: Kestrels can often be seen hover-hunting; they hover on rapidly beating wings while hunting for prey. They can also be seen sitting upright on wires and posts. They cache food to eat later.

American Kestrel adult female   Photo by Ned Harris

Voice: The Kestrel has a rapid, shrill "klee-klee-klee" call. It sounds very much like a person calling "kitty, kitty, kitty"!

Nesting: Kestrels are cavity nesters. They use bird boxes, natural cavities in dead portions of trees, or old woodpecker nest sites. They add little or no nesting material to the cavity. The female lays four to five white eggs with brownish markings at two- to three-day intervals. She does most of the incubating, during which time the male feeds her and stands guard against intruders. The eggs hatch in about a month. The young are tended by both parents and fledge about a month after hatching.

Kestrels only have one brood per year, unless it is an exceptionally food-rich year, in which case they may have two.

Food: The Kestrel predominantly feeds on small rodents and lizards. It also takes large insects and, occasionally, small birds.

Will they use my yard? Kestrels are common in the Inland Empire. They frequent yards that are on the urban fringe, adjacent to open country. Kestrels can be seen along roadsides and in fields wherever there are perches, such as telephone lines and fence posts, to hunt from.

Key things to look for:
1) Robin-sized. **2)** Long, pointed wings. **3)** Long tail. **4)** Hover-hunts. **5)** Two black vertical stripes on face.

American Kestrel adult male

APPENDICES

LOOK-ALIKES

Hummingbird Females and Immatures

Costa's Hummingbird

Black-chinned Hummingbird   *Anna's Hummingbird*   Photo by Charles Melton

159

Hawks in Flight and Immatures

Red-tailed Hawk immature

Cooper's Hawk immature

Red-shouldered Hawk immature

Red-shouldered Hawk immature

Cooper's Hawk immature

Oriole and Tanager Females and Immatures

Hooded Oriole female

Hooded Oriole juvenile

Bullock's Oriole female

Western Tanager female

Bullock's Oriole male with first-year plumage

Sparrow, Finch, Starling, and Grosbeak Females and Immatures

House Finch female

Pine Siskin

Song Sparrow

White-crowned Sparrow juvenile

House Sparrow male in nonbreeding plumage   *House Sparrow female*

European Starling juvenile   *Black-headed Grosbeak female*

Dark Birds

Brown-headed Cowbird male

European Starling adult in breeding plumage

Brewer's Blackbird male

California Towhee

Brewer's Blackbird female

Brown-headed Cowbird female

UNUSUAL BIRDS
YOU MIGHT SEE IN YOUR YARD

No bird book could deal with every bird that might come through your yard, but I have created a list of those that have been reported to occasionally visit yards in the Inland Empire. These sightings are made primarily during migration or in yards adjacent to a "natural" area. But wherever you are, keep your eyes open! This list will help narrow down your choices so that you can refer to a field guide more easily.

Permanent Residents, but "Edge Species"

Great Egret	If you have a fishpond in your yard.
Great Blue Heron	If you have a fishpond in your yard.
Western Kingbird	Usually likes open fields with some trees nearby.
California Quail	If you live next to a large "natural" area such as Box Springs or Sycamore Canyon.
Common Raven	
Loggerhead Shrike	If you live near a large, open, grassy area, such as the Box Springs Mountains or agricultural fields.
California Thrasher	
Downy Woodpecker	Tends to occur in riparian areas.
Cactus Wren	If you have large patches of cactus on your property or nearby.
Rock Wren	If you live near a rocky area.
Canyon Wren	If you live near dry, open areas, canyons, and cliffs, such as the Box Springs Mountains.

Winter Visitors Only

Mountain Chickadee	Usually occurs in pines at higher elevations.
White-breasted Nuthatch	Usually occurs at higher elevations in the local mountains.
Purple Finch	
Blue-gray Gnatcatcher	
Sharp-shinned Hawk	
Merlin	
Red-breasted Sapsucker	
Chipping Sparrow	
Golden-crowned Sparrow	
Fox Sparrow	
Lark Sparrow	

Migrants

Ash-throated Flycatcher	Usually just a migrant on its way to riparian areas, although some do nest here, especially along the Santa Ana River.
Pacific-slope Flycatcher	
Allen's Hummingbird	
Rufous Hummingbird	
Western Wood Pewee	
Say's Phoebe	Fall and winter visitor; prefers dry, open areas, canyons, and cliffs.
Rough-winged Swallow	
Tree Swallow	
Violet-Green Swallow	
Swainson's Thrush	
Solitary Vireo	

MacGillivray's Warbler

Nashville Warbler

Townsend's Warbler

Yellow Warbler

Visitors

Barn Swallow	Breeding visitor, prefers to nest under bridges and in culverts.

ATTRACTING BIRDS
TO YOUR YARD

Attracting birds to your yard can be a fun challenge. It can provide a wonderful connection with nature and help you learn about other species, without even having to leave the comfort of your home! One of the most wonderful things about living in southern California is our opportunity to study and learn about different birds all year long.

Plan Your "Birdscape"

Plan your habitat, considering the horizontal as well as the vertical space you will landscape, or "birdscape." You have the horizontal space of your lot, so start with a map, drawing, or aerial photo to help measure what space you have, and what you might fit in it. You also have a vertical space, or cross-section, from ground level to treetops. The vertical area includes:

1) The soil (basement)
2) The low-growing plants (or ground floor)

Example of a "birdscape"   Illustration by Melissa Badalian

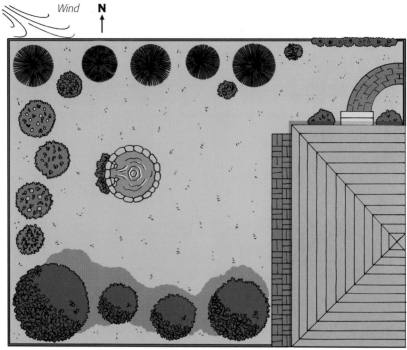

Deciduous trees provide shade during the summer. Illustration by Melissa Badalian
Evergreen trees provide year-round shelter from prevailing winds.

3) The understory of shrubs, vines, and smaller trees

4) The tree canopy, or large trees

- **To start your birdscape plan, identify existing plants** in your yard. Determine how much shade and protection the trees and shrubs provide, and if they provide a valuable food source.

- **Do your (bird) research.** Where you live will determine what birds you might attract. Observe your neighborhood and use this book to determine which birds could be attracted to your yard. If you live on the edge of the city or next to a park, you will probably be able to attract a larger variety of birds than if you live in an area surrounded by buildings.

  Bird species vary in their habits. Some prefer deeply wooded spaces, while others like open fields. They live and depend on one or more of the vertical vegetation levels. The Western Bluebird, for example, uses open fields for finding and feeding on insects, yet nests in tree cavities.

- **Draw your yard,** including important features such as existing structures, water sources, pathways, utilities, and plants. Include the features and effects of neighboring properties, such as shared walls or trees that overhang and shade portions of your yard.
- **Considering the site constraints,** make alterations to your drawing, adding and, if necessary, removing trees, shrubs, grasses, or ground covers to improve habitat quality. Trees and shrubs are very important because they provide shelter and serve as the framework for the landscape. However, consider eventual plant size and placement. For example, placing deciduous trees (trees that drop their leaves) southwest of your house will provide cooling shade in summer but allow in warming sunshine during winter. Plant evergreen trees and shrubs in a location where they will help slow prevailing winds and provide year-round shelter.

"Birdscaping" Suggestions

In order to attract birds, you need to have a basic understanding of their needs for food, water, nesting sites, and shelter.

Water

In southern California the most critical need for birds is water. Due to long, usually rainless summers, birds must find water where they can, both for drinking and for bathing. A water source attracts more birds than any other feature. Birds such as insect eaters that may not visit feeders will regularly take advantage of water.

Birds need water year-round, not just during summer months. I found this out one winter. I had placed a small cereal bowl of water for my cat on top of my six-foot-high patio wall. One weekend morning I noticed a Yellow-rumped Warbler drinking from it. A little later, a flock of Cedar Waxwings flew in to use the bowl for bathing and drinking. They were followed by a flock of Western Bluebirds! I placed several additional bowls on the wall, which were equally well used. This continued all winter, and the flocks returned each winter after that.

Fortunately, providing water is one of the easiest ways to attract birds to your yard.

Photo by Sheila Kee

- Moving water is preferred and can easily be provided with a dripper or a mister. A circulating pump can be added to a birdbath or pond to create movement.

- Shallow water, one to two inches deep, allows birds to immerse themselves to bathe and cool off. Any type of container can be used as a birdbath: a shallow saucer, a deeper bowl filled with rocks, or a boulder with a shallow depression that holds water.

- It's a good idea to place several different types of birdbaths in your yard; put one on the ground and one on an elevated pedestal. Place the water away from dense vegetation if cats, other mammals, or predatory birds might be a problem. Low fencing around water sources can be constructed to deter predators and allow time for birds to escape.

I have several water spots in my yard. I place a shallow, large, ceramic plate (one that is sold to put under large flowerpots) on the ground under my outdoor faucet. I then let the faucet drip very slowly into the plate. Some birds love to hang off the faucet head to drink, while others drink and bathe in the plate. The plate is in an open area, but with escape cover within ten feet. I also have a watering plate on top of my patio roof for those birds that do not like to venture too close to the ground. These

Rock with shallow depression that holds water   Photo by Sheila Kee

include the Scrub Jays, Mockingbirds, and Western Bluebirds. I have even had a Northern Flicker come to this watering hole.

Food

Although many people use feeders to provide food for birds, the most natural way is to landscape with appropriate food-bearing plants. In the long run, it is much simpler than continually stocking a feeder, plus it provides food for birds that do not use feeders. With forethought, you can plant a garden that will feed birds throughout the year. Some species of birds are year-round residents, while others overwinter or migrate through the Inland Empire. We get many winter visitors that have different food requirements from our summer birds.

To attract birds, *plant a variety of food sources.* "Mix it up" in terms of plant species and plant heights to provide a variety of food for all times of the year, and to provide shelter and escape from predators. Select plants that flower and bear fruit at different times of the year.

Unlike most other species, hummingbirds, our tiniest birds, rely on nectar as a primary source of food. Hummingbirds are attracted to a wide variety of nectar-producing plants, especially those that have red or

Acorn Woodpecker at granary tree

purple tubular flowers. Many of these plants, such as penstemons and sages, grow well in the Inland Empire climate.

Select native and drought-tolerant plant species whenever possible. Natives are adapted to the local climate, soils, and wildlife. Since native plants are adapted to having no or low amounts of summer water, try to group natives and drought-tolerant plants together in areas that will get less irrigation. For example, native oak trees, such as *Quercus agrifolia,* are one of the most valuable wildlife food sources. (Acorn Woodpeckers, Band-tailed Pigeons, and Scrub Jays eat the acorns. Warblers, finches, woodpeckers, and many other birds eat the insects that inhabit the oak.) However, our native oaks are difficult to keep disease-free if planted in heavily irrigated lawns.

One of the best ways to attract birds is to let your yard be as natural or "wild" as possible—in other words, not too well-manicured. For example, let some grasses mature to seed. Plant native wildflowers or other flowering annuals, such as sunflowers, coneflowers, and lupine. Allow annuals to go to seed, and leave the dry plant residues. Let shrubs grow into thickets. Allow fallen tree branches and leaf litter to remain and decay naturally. In place of edged, straight lines, plant in curves and clumps, creating hidden retreats for animals. Neatly mowed, grassy front yards provide little habitat for most birds. Unfortunately, one of the birds that thrives in groomed yards is the Starling, pest to both humans and other birds.

At the end of this Appendix, you will find a list of local birds and their food preferences and a list of plants that provide those foods. The plants are grouped according to what type of food they provide:

- Seeds and nuts
- Fruits and berries

Food for hummingbirds   Photo by Sheila Kee

- Nectar
- Insects (the plants support insects and create insect habitat)

Select items from each list to create a diverse habitat.

There are many books written on the popular subject of gardening for wildlife; however, most are written for an eastern United States audience. Consult with local nurseries and gardens that specialize in growing native and drought-tolerant plants, such as: Mockingbird Nursery (Riverside); Tree of Life Nursery (San Juan Capistrano); Rancho Santa Ana Botanic Gardens (Claremont); Theodore Payne Foundation for Wildflowers and Native Plants (Sun Valley); Landscapes Southern California Style (Riverside); and University of California Riverside Botanic Gardens.

Supplemental Food

If you decide to take on the responsibility to provide supplemental food for birds, here are some suggestions for planning a feeding station. The ideal feeding station might include a variety of feeder styles at different elevations, with shelter from wind and predators.

Provide a safe environment where birds can easily escape, should a predator approach, and where cats and other predators cannot lie in wait.

Strategically place feeders in relation to walls, roofs, trees, fences, thick, thorny shrubs, and brush piles.

Provide desirable foods in safe and appropriate feeders. Learn about the food habits of the neighborhood birds and of the birds you plan to attract. If you decide to provide feeders, provide several types with a variety of seeds and mixtures, especially black oil and striped sunflower seeds, thistle, peanuts, and millet (red or white). Less desirable seeds are cracked corn (attracts Starlings and Crows) and milo (not a favorite of many birds).

Many styles of feeders are available on the market, each one geared toward a specific need. There are feeder trays for ground-feeding birds, thistle feeders for finches, suet feeders, and more. Look for feeders made of durable materials that are easy to fill and clean. Some seedeaters, such as Mourning Doves and Quail, prefer not to use feeders, but eat on or near the ground. Rotate ground-feeding areas.

You can also make feeders from things around the house, but don't use treated wood. Almost anything can be a feeder; an upturned garbage can lid, a stump, or a plastic bottle. Be creative! There are many books and magazine articles available with suggestions.

Clean feeders of old and moldy seed. Scrub feeders and soak in a light solution of 9 parts water to 1 part bleach. Rinse well and dry. To avoid contamination, limit ground feeding below hanging feeders or perches. Spread mulch below feeders, then rake and remove with the accumulated droppings and hulls.

Be consistent in keeping feeders filled, especially during harsh weather. If you wish to feed only in winter, start early in fall and continue well into spring, until you notice a reduction in the amount of food consumed. Birds raise their young in the springtime and need to provide food for them in addition to feeding themselves.

Remember, not all birds are seedeaters and not all will use bird feeders. Insect eating birds, such as woodpeckers, are attracted to shrubs and trees for the insects that they provide. Leaf litter under shrubs and trees provides insect habitat for ground-feeding insect eaters, such as the California Towhee. You can also provide live food, such as mealworms, which can be purchased at pet and bait stores.

Attract fruit and berry eaters, such as Mockingbirds, Cedar Waxwings, and Robins, by placing fresh fruit on or nailing it to trays or feeding tables. Many birds enjoy chopped or halved oranges, apples, bananas, and raisins.

Orioles will struggle to use hummingbird feeders; however, specially designed oriole feeders are available, which makes feeding easier for them. Hummingbirds and orioles are attracted to feeders of sugar water. Mix one cup boiling water to ¼ cup of sugar (4 parts water to 1 part sugar). Change the sugar water every two to three days, especially when the temperatures are warm. *Please* clean out your hummingbird and oriole feeders, using only hot water and a little detergent, no bleach, at least once a week to remove any harmful mold, mildew, or fungus. Avoid using food coloring. Never use honey or artificial sweeteners.

Shelter and Nesting Sites

For winter shelter, plant evergreen hedges and trees, preferably at the northern edge of your yard—if planted in a southwest location, evergreens could shade a yard or home during the cool winter months. Deciduous trees in a southwestern location will allow the warm sunlight in during the cooler months.

If you have dead and hollow trees, consider leaving them for perches, nesting sites, and protection for birds, unless they pose a hazard. Many people are not aware of the value of dead, dying, and hollow trees, as well as logs on the ground. You might also construct log, rock, or brush piles to provide cover.

Constructed Shelter   Illustration by Melissa Badalian

During the breeding season, birds will evaluate your yard for nesting potential. Most birds have specific nesting requirements, so your yard may be limited as to which types it can support.

Cavity Nesters: Some birds are cavity nesters; in other words, they use holes in large tree trunks or branches. Some, such as woodpeckers, excavate their own holes. Others, Starlings and House Wrens for example, use other birds' homes or openings that occur naturally, such as crevices.

Nest Boxes: Most cavity nesters will use nest boxes.

- The sizes of both the nest box and entrance hole vary by species, so be sure to read one of the many books available on the subject for all the details. *It is very important to use boxes with the correct entrance hole size for the birds you are trying to attract.* If you make the entrance hole too large, the box will probably be taken over by Starlings instead of native species.

- Make sure to place nest boxes in a species' preferred habitat. For example, put boxes for House Wrens and Bewick's Wrens in bushes and put Kestrel boxes high above open areas.

- When planning or purchasing nest boxes, consider the ease of hanging and lowering them for cleaning. It will be important to remove old nests in the fall after breeding season is finished. Leave boxes in place year-round, since some species use them as roosting sites during winter.

- Consider how and where the boxes will be mounted to protect against predators. By providing habitat, we may be unwittingly providing prey for other animals, such as cats, raccoons, and opossums. Predators, including jays, crows, and owls, will seek out nesting birds, nestlings, even eggs, so consider using metal baffles under nest boxes and placing boxes on poles.

Have patience! You may have immediate success, or it may take several seasons before birds move into your nest box.

Open-cup nesters: Many birds are referred to as "open-cup nesters." These birds build open, cup-shaped nests among the leaves and branches of trees and shrubs. Although in the open, these birds still need the protection of foliage while they raise their young. One of the worst things

Nest box ·   Photo by Sheila Kee

you can do is prune trees and shrubs during nesting season. By doing so, you may reduce the number of birds that will find your yard attractive for nesting, and you could inadvertently cause harm to the young.

If you do prune and end up removing an active nest, try to lodge it back into the tree as near as possible to where it was originally. If the nest is destroyed, line a small cardboard box with soft material and secure it in the tree or shrub. The parents usually will not abandon the young and will continue to feed them if left alone. People often think that if a human has handled the young, the parents will not return to care for them. This applies to mammals, but not to birds. Bird species actually have a poor sense of smell. However, do not handle a nest any more than is necessary, as predators may follow the human scent to it.

If you find truly abandoned baby or injured birds, contact a local licensed wildlife rehabilitator. Refer to the California Council for Wildlife Rehabilitators' website at www.ccwr.org. Look under "Resources," "Regional Listings," and then "Region 5," or call the Humane Society or a local pet store.

Birder Ethics and Potential Human Impacts

It is exciting to find a nest, but please do not disturb the occupants! Many birds will abandon their nests if they are disturbed at critical times, particularly in the early stages of laying and incubation. In addition, the nestlings, if disturbed, may leave the nest before they are able to fly. This puts them at great risk of being taken by cats or predatory birds. So enjoy the nest and its activities from a distance, with a pair of binoculars. Often the best view is from your own window, since the house can serve as a "blind."

When we decide to invite birds into our yards, we assume part of the responsibility for their survival. Sometimes human interaction can create problems. So it's up to us to correct and prevent whatever problems we possibly can. For example, when a hummingbird feeder is not kept clean, a deadly fungus may begin growing in the sugar water. This "human-created" problem, providing a food source without keeping the feeder clean, would be a disservice.

Here are some other examples of human impacts and ways to reduce them:

- If you live on the edge of open space, especially riparian (waterway) habitat, your property management will have an even greater impact on birds and wildlife. Reduce light, noise, and other activities that disturb wildlife. Do not allow pets to disturb wildlife, and do not allow pets to roam in open spaces.

- Exercise care when using pesticides, herbicides, and fertilizers. Not only can they impact your immediate yard, but they will enter runoff and waterways if not properly applied. Practice least toxic backyard and home management by minimizing chemical use.

For insect control, try appropriate treatments, such as beneficial insects, birds, bats, insecticidal soaps, horticultural oils, traps, sulfur dust, etc. Avoid using insecticides other than the "natural" ones, such as those containing pyrethrins, nicotine, or rotenone. These are among the safest. Those containing dieldrin, endrin, aldrin, toxaphene, and heptachlor should be totally avoided. Please, read the labels before buying and using any insecticides!

For more information about sustainable and environmentally safe yard management and more, request a free copy of "Living on the Edge" from the Riverside-Corona Resource Conservation District at (951) 683-7691.

Cats: Personally, I love, and own, cats, but they are one of the worst enemies of birds because they are skillful hunters. Cats can greatly reduce some bird populations, especially those that feed on, or close to, the ground.

Cats are particularly harmful to birds in the springtime when the young are in the nest or just learning to fly. There is nothing sadder to see than your cat at the back door with a baby bird in its mouth. If at all possible, keep your cat inside, at least in the spring. You might fence off an area just for birds, so that cats would have a difficult time getting to them. Some people put bells on their pets' collars and keep them inside early in the morning and late in the evening, when many birds are active and feeding.

You will need to be creative to keep cats from getting the birds in your yard. Be aware, this can be a real problem! If you cannot significantly reduce the cat problem, you may have to forgo attracting birds to your yard.

For information about attracting birds and wildlife to your yard, contact the Riverside-Corona Resource Conservation District and request "Wild about Natives," "Living on the Edge," "Backyard Conservation," various nest box drawings, a list of beneficial insect suppliers, and more at (951) 683-7691, ext. 207. Also, visit www.rcrcd.com.

FOOD PREFERENCES
OF INLAND EMPIRE BIRDS

Western Scrub Jay   Photo by Sheila Kee

I have included this guide to help you know which of the more common birds will be attracted by what food sources.

- Fruit eaters are attracted to fruit trees in the summer (so be prepared to share!) and berry-producing shrubs in the fall and winter. Orioles are attracted to sugar-water feeders and orange or grapefruit halves put out for them. Other fruit eating species are attracted to suet.

- Meat eaters are more likely to be attracted to water you provide in your yard.

- Insect eaters can easily be attracted to your yard by providing suet, mealworms, and water sources.

- Seedeaters, overall, are most attracted to black oil sunflowers seeds. Ground-feeding seedeaters are attracted to white proso millet. Finches prefer thistle. If you purchase commercial bird feed that includes seeds other than these, chances are you will be wasting your money: in the short run, these commercial birdseed mixes may seem less expensive, but they are mostly "filler." You may end up making a mess, as the birds will toss the filler seed out of the feeder. Even worse, if the spilled seed becomes damp and develops fungus and mold, it may contribute to bird disease.

You will find the birds marked with an asterisk (*) on more than one of the following lists. When these birds are in the Inland Empire they will eat fairly equal quantities from each of the lists on which they appear.

Fruit and Berry Eaters (7 species)

American Robin*

Black-headed Grosbeak*

Cedar Waxwing

Hooded Oriole*

House Finch*

Northern Mockingbird

Western Bluebird*

Meat Eaters (9 species)

American Kestrel

American Robin*

Barn Owl

Cooper's Hawk

Great Horned Owl

Greater Roadrunner

Red-shouldered Hawk

Red-tailed Hawk

Insect Eaters (20 species)

Bewick's Wren

Black Phoebe

Black-throated Gray Warbler

Brewer's Blackbird

Brown-headed Cowbird

Bullock's Oriole

Bushtit

Cliff Swallow

Hermit Thrush

Hooded Oriole*

House Wren

Killdeer

Northern Flicker

Nuttall's Woodpecker

Orange-crowned Warbler

Phainopepla

Ruby-crowned Kinglet

Western Bluebird*

Wilson's Warbler

Yellow-rumped Warbler

Photo by Sheila Kee

Nectar Feeders (4 species)

Anna's Hummingbird

Black-chinned Hummingbird

Costa's Hummingbird

Hooded Oriole*

Seed and Nut Eaters (14 species)

Acorn Woodpecker

American Goldfinch

Band-tailed Pigeon

Black-headed Grosbeak*

California Towhee

Dark-eyed Junco

House Finch*

Lesser Goldfinch

Mourning Dove

Pine Siskin

Rock Dove

Spotted Towhee

Western Scrub Jay

Wilson's Warbler

Scavengers (4 species)

American Crow

Common Raven

European Starling

House Sparrow

PLANTS FOR
ATTRACTING BIRDS

If you are interested in attracting birds to your yard or garden, here are some suggestions for the Inland Empire. To learn more about a plant's growth requirements, check the Sunset *Western Garden Book,* an excellent reference.

Plants for Seed and Nut Eating Birds

Common Name	Scientific Name	Growth Habit
Pine	*Pinus* spp.	tree
Oak	*Quercus* spp.	tree
White Alder	*Alnus rhombifolia*	tree
California Sycamore	*Platanus racemosa*	tree
Sweet Gum	*Liquidambar* spp.	tree
Cosmos	*Cosmos*	annual (self-seeding)
Coreopsis	*Coreopsis*	perennial and annual
Sunflowers	*Helianthus annuus*	annual (self-seeding)
Mexican Sunflower	*Tithonia rotundifolia*	perennial grown as annual
Mullein	*Verbascum* spp.	biennial, perennial
Coneflower	*Echinacea* spp.	perennial (self-seeding)

Plants for Fruit Eating Birds

Common Name	Scientific Name	Growth Habit
Fruits, such as apricot, plum, nectarine, peach		tree
Berries, such as blackberry and raspberry		vine
Silk Tassel	*Garrya elliptica*	tree
Elderberry	*Sambucus* spp.	tree
Edible Fig	*Ficus carica*	tree
Fruiting Mulberry	*Morus alba*	tree
Fruiting Crabapple		tree
Olive	*Olea europaea*	tree
Strawberry Tree	*Arbutus unedo*	tree
Crape Myrtle	*Lagerstroemia indica*	tree or shrub
Wild Lilac	*Ceanothus* spp.	shrub, ground cover
Currant, Gooseberry	*Ribes* spp.	shrub
Toyon	*Heteromeles arbutifolia*	large shrub
Holly-leaf Redberry	*Rhamnus crocea ilicifolia*	shrub
Coffeeberry	*Rhamnus californica*	shrub
Lemonade Berry	*Rhus integrifolia*	shrub
Sugarbush	*Rhus ovata*	shrub
Cotoneaster	Avoid: *Cotoneaster parneyi*	shrub
Holly	*Ilex altaclarensis* "Wilsonii" or *Ilex comuta* "Burfordii"	shrub, small tree shrub
Juniper	*Juniperus* spp.	shrub, small tree
Natal Plum	*Carissa grandiflora*	shrub
Bush Honeysuckles	*Lonicera* spp.	shrub
Summer Holly	*Comarostaphylis diversifolia*	shrub
California Holly Grape	*Mahonia pinnata*	shrub
Roses	*Rosa* spp.	shrub

Plants for Nectar Feeding Birds

Common Name	Scientific Name	Growth Habit
Flowering Quince	*Chaenomeles* spp.	tree
Bottlebrush	*Callistemon citrinus* or *Callistemon lanceolatus*	tree
Silk Oak Tree	*Grevillea robusta*	tree
Acacia	*Acacia* spp.	tree
Silk Tree	*Albizia* spp.	tree
Butterfly Bush	*Buddleia* spp.	shrub
Melaleuca	*Melaleuca leucadendra*	shrub
Wooly Grevillea	*Grevillea lanigera*	shrub
Bird of Paradise Bush	*Caesalpinia gilliesii*	shrub
Currant, Gooseberry	*Ribes* spp.	shrub
Sages	*Salvia* spp.	shrub
Bee Balm	*Monarda* spp.	shrub
Red Hot Poker	*Kniphofia uvaria*	perennial
Aloes	*Aloe* spp.	succulent
Monkey Flower	*Mimulus* spp.	perennial
Honeysuckle	*Lonicera* spp.	shrub or vine
Fairy Duster	*Calliandra eriophylla*	shrub
Summer Holly	*Comarostaphylis diversifolia*	shrub
California Fuchsia	*Zauschneria* spp.	shrub
Shrimp Plant	*Justicia californica*	shrub
Cardinal Flower	*Lobelia cardinalis*	shrub
California Holly Grape	*Mahonia pinnata*	shrub
Ipomopsis	*Ipomopsis* spp.	biennial or perennial
Lemonade Berry	*Rhus integrifolia*	shrub
Sugarbush	*Rhus ovata*	shrub

Plants for Nectar Feeding Birds, *continued*

Common Name	Scientific Name	Growth Habit
Wooly Blue Curls	*Trichostema lanatum*	perennial
Coral Bells	*Heuchera* spp.	perennial
Beard Tongue	*Penstemon* spp.	perennial
Foxglove	*Digitalis* spp.	biennial or perennial
Impatiens	*Impatiens* spp.	perennial or annual
Larkspur	*Delphinium* spp.	perennial or annual

Plants for Insect Eating Birds

Common Name	Scientific Name	Growth Habit
Oak	*Quercus* spp.	tree
Pine	*Pinus* spp.	tree
Silk Tree	*Albizia* spp.	tree
Birch	*Betula* spp.	tree
California Sycamore	*Platanus racemosa*	tree
Acacia	*Acacia* spp.	tree
Silk Tassel	*Garrya elliptica*	tree
Bottlebrush	*Callistemon citrinus* or *Callistemon lanceolatus*	tree
Butterfly Bush	*Buddleia* spp.	shrub
Melaleuca	*Melaleuca leucadendra*	shrub

APPENDIX D

WHAT ELSE CAN I DO?

Activities to Help You Learn More

Observe!

1. Now that you are learning the birds in your own yard, begin noticing where else you see them—in a nearby park, near your workplace, places you visit on vacation. Remember that many of these birds have a range that may extend into other habitats and regions of California, into other states, and even into other countries. You can learn the range of each individual species in most field guides.

2. If your friends have different birds in their yards than you, try to figure out why. Are you closer to a natural area? Do they have water in their yards? Do you have denser vegetation? Do they have no cats in the immediate neighborhood? What else could contribute to the difference in bird species you and your friends have?

3. Begin noticing how different birds look. Notice that birds in the same family are more alike in appearance and behavior than those in different families. For instance, the House Wren and Bewick's Wren are in the same family. Notice the similar bill shape and size. Notice similar behaviors. Now notice how birds of the Wren family look different than birds of the Sparrow family. Notice the differences in bill shape and size. Notice the differences in behaviors.

Listen!

1. Begin learning the songs and calls of the birds you see most frequently in your yard. You'll be amazed at how much it helps you know what birds are around. Start with just one bird, the most common in your yard. Now focus on this bird for a short while (even a few minutes)

and listen to the calls and songs it makes. Every time you see this bird, listen for its calls and song until you are able to identify it just by hearing it. Then move on to another common backyard bird and do the same. Over time you can add more birds, until you find that you *are* "birding," without even seeing the birds. Try this sometime when you just wake up and are still in bed—see how many birds you can identify without seeing them!

Think!

1. Think about why the females of most species are duller in color. Why are the young duller in color?

2. Think about why different bird species and families have different bill shapes. Why do some have short, conical bills and others have thin bills or curved bills? Hint: relate their bill shapes to what they eat.

3. If you have a particular bird you enjoy watching, let that draw you into learning more about it. What are its habits? What is its distribution? Does it occur only in California or in the U.S.? Can it be found anywhere else in the world? What other birds are in its family? What are their similarities? What are their differences?

4. What roles have birds played in people's lives through the centuries, or in different cultures? What myths have been created around birds?

Places and Organizations to Help You Learn More

Are you hooked now? Are you thinking, "What else can I do?" Well, here's a list of organizations that are always looking for new members and volunteers and/or provide local activities to help increase your bird skills and knowledge. Have fun! But remember, the more you learn, the more addicted you get!

National Audubon Society: This is a national association, but most areas have their own local chapters. Check www.audubon.org, "Birds & Science," for information about projects, including bird conservation issues, bird activities for kids, and travel.

The National Audubon Society conducts yearly **Christmas Bird Counts**, where groups of birders spend the day counting all the birds they see and hear within a designated area. Even if you are a beginner, the help of "extra eyes" is always welcome in finding birds others may not have seen.

The Audubon Society's Inland Empire chapter is the **San Bernardino Valley Audubon Society** (SBVAS). Join the SBVAS even if you don't want to join the national organization. The SBVAS has monthly slide shows, a monthly newsletter, and lots of birding field trips throughout the year. At the monthly meetings you will find a great variety of bird books and other natural history books, plus birding paraphernalia, for sale. The SBVAS usually meets at the San Bernardino County Museum, 2024 Orange Tree Lane, Redlands, CA 92374. See www.sbvas.org for more information.

A great place to get acquainted with birding books is the **Los Angeles Audubon Bookstore.** You can call (323) 876-0202 and request a catalog, or order online through the website, www.LosAngelesAudubon.org. The catalog lists books on particular bird species and birding areas, ranging from local to worldwide. This is a great way to find books that are not usually carried in our local bookstores. They also sell binoculars, feeders, videos, and much more.

Pomona Valley Audubon Society has a website, www. PomonaValley-Audubon.org.

The San Jacinto Wildlife Area offers beginning bird trips. Find out more at www. sjwa.info or 17050 Davis Road, Lakeview, CA 92567.

The **University of California Extension** offers beginning bird classes, usually in the spring and fall. For information about classes, call (951) 827-4105 or go to http://www.extension.ucr.edu.

The **San Bernardino County Museum** has a permanent collection of mounted birds and the fourth-largest collection of bird eggs in the world. The museum also has a gift shop where you can find all types of natural history and bird-related items. The museum is located off the I-10 freeway at 2024 Orange Tree Lane in Redlands. Call (909) 307-2669 for hours.

The **Riverside Metropolitan Museum** has interesting dioramas that depict local habitats with plant and animal specimens. The museum runs a "Nature Lab" of natural history activities for the whole family and operates a gift shop. It is located at 3580 Mission Inn Avenue in downtown Riverside. Call (951) 826-5273 for hours.

The **Laboratory of Ornithology at Cornell University** has Citizen Science activities for people with all levels of skill. The lab coordinates Project FeederWatch, the Great Backyard Bird Count, the Backyard Wildlife Habitat Program, the Nest Box Network, and Classroom FeederWatch. You can get involved in any of these projects by contacting Cornell Lab of Ornithology, Project Services, 159 Sapsucker Woods Road, Ithaca, NY 14850. Or call 1 (800) 843-BIRD (2473) to request a registration form. Their website can be found at birds.cornell.edu.

National Wildlife Federation (NWF) has a Backyard Wildlife Habitat program. If you provide food, water, shelter, and places for birds to raise their young, your yard can become certified as a true wildlife habitat! You can contact NWF at 1 (800) 822-9919 to request an information packet, or learn about the program at www.nwf.org/backyard.

The **California Native Plant Society** has an Inland Empire chapter where you can learn about landscaping with native plants that provide habitat for native birds. Statewide CNPS information is at www.cnps.org or (916) 447-2677. The local Riverside–San Bernardino chapter has a newsletter, "The Encelia," that can also be accessed at www.cnps.org.

Rancho Santa Ana Botanic Garden (RSABG) is the largest botanical garden dedicated exclusively to California's native plants. RSABG is near the Claremont Colleges. Visit RSABG at 1500 No. College Avenue, Claremont, CA 91711 to learn about landscaping with California native plants that provide habitat for birds. See rsabg.org for more information. RSABG has a hotline to call with questions about native plants, (909) 624-0838.

Landscapes Southern California Style is a water conservation garden at Western Municipal Water District. See www.wmwd.com/landscape.htm to learn about landscaping with drought-tolerant habitat plants. The garden is located at 450 East Alessandro Blvd., Riverside, CA 92505, (951) 789-5036.

The **University of California Riverside Botanic Gardens** have a bird list and lots of trails to take at your leisure. To get to the trails, enter the UCR campus and follow signs to the Botanic Gardens. For more information, call (951) 784-6962.

The **Riverside-Corona Resource Conservation District** is a local government agency that helps conserve natural resources by providing information to land-users and by coordinating community efforts. To request free technical information or to volunteer for local conservation projects, such as the Bluebird Trail (hanging and monitoring nest boxes in spring), waterway cleanups, or invasive species removal, please contact the Riverside-Corona Resource Conservation District office at (951) 683-7691, www.RCRCD.com.

There are also an unlimited number of websites dedicated to just about every imaginable bird interest. There are websites for specific birds, such as hummingbirds, woodpeckers, raptors, chickadees, and on and on.

The Birder Home Page at www.birder.com has information for beginners and advanced birders alike, including links to bird hot spots, bird photos, and birdcalls.

The **North American Bluebird Society** can be contacted at www. nablue birdsociety.org or phone (812) 988-1876.

Enature, at www.enature.com, offers online searchable field guides to over 4,800 plant and animal species. Derived from thirty-five different Audubon Society field guides, regional guides, and nature guides, the database is keyword-searchable by group (mammals, amphibians, fishes, trees, etc.) or browsable within subheadings for each group.

The **California Council for Wildlife Rehabilitators'** website is located at www.ccwr.org. Look under Resources, Regional Listings, and then Region 5 to find certified wildlife rehabilitators.

Also, see BeWaterWise.com for a **California Friendly Gardening Guide** and much more.

References and Suggested Reading

Bent, Arthur C. Life Histories of North American Birds series. The eighteen books in this series are absolute classics—written from the 1930s to the 1950s—and are a must-read, both for the wealth of information about each bird species and for the wonderful "romantic" style of writing (unlike the scientific style of today). But be forewarned, the species' common names (and some of the scientific names) have changed over the years. So it may take some time to figure out exactly what species' accounts to read.

Childs, Henry E. Jr. *Where Birders Go in Southern California* (Los Angeles: Los Angeles Audubon Society, 1993). This book is divided by county and includes a numbered county map that correlates with written directions to each viewing spot. It gives very precise locations for finding specific species.

Ehrlich, Paul R., David S. Dobkin, and Darryl Wheye. *The Birder's Handbook: A Field Guide to the Natural History of North American Birds* (New York: Simon and Schuster, 1988). This is a great book for basic information about every bird species in North America. It provides short synopses of relevant material, from nesting information to diet. There is also a lot of valuable information throughout the book on many subjects relating to birds: migration, behaviors, etc. A must for your bookshelf!

Fisher, Chris C., and Herbert Clarke. *Birds of Los Angeles: Including Santa Barbara, Ventura and Orange Counties* (Renton, WA: Lone Pine Publishing, 1997). This book is one of many available to help you expand your birding adventures beyond the Riverside area. It suggests common birds that you can see in all types of habitats.

Garrett, Kimball, and Jon Dunn. *Birds of Southern California: Status and Distribution* (Los Angeles: Los Angeles Audubon Society, 1981). This book gives great information on our southern California birds and their habitat range of distribution. It includes all birds known to occur in southern California.

Harrison, Colin. *A Field Guide to the Nests, Eggs and Nestlings of North American Birds* (Brattleboro, VT: Stephen Greene Press, 1978). One of several good nest books, this field guide gives you details about the nests themselves, what the eggs look like (with lots of pictures), and pictures of nestlings of some bird species.

Harrison, Hal H. *A Field Guide to Western Birds' Nests* (Boston: Houghton Mifflin Harcourt, 2001). This is another good book on bird nests. It has photographs of almost all the birds' nests, in addition to information about the nests and eggs.

Lee, Cin-Ty. *Birdwatching in Riverside, California: Dedicated to Young Birders in the Riverside Area and Beyond* (Redlands, CA: San Bernardino County Museum Association, 1995). This is a great book about birds in our local area, to help you expand beyond your own yard. It includes parks, campuses, and wildlife areas. It lets you know exactly where to go and what to expect to see when you get there. It also has very useful information to get you started on birding.

Small, Arnold. *California Birds: Their Status and Distribution* (Vista, CA: Ibis Publishing, 1994). This is a wonderful book, specific to birds that occur in California. It gives information about seasonal status, habitat, and range in California, providing a good way to learn about the birds in our area, from the common ones to the rare ones.

Terres, John K. *The Audubon Society Encyclopedia of North American Birds* (New York: Wings Books,1980). I can't say enough about this book. It is the ultimate resource for birders at all skill levels. It is set up similarly to a dictionary but gives detailed information about every aspect of bird behavior, physical appearance, individual bird species, etc. This book can probably answer just about any question you might have about birds. Amazingly, I often see this book on the bargain table at the bookstores, so you can find it at a good price, too.

GLOSSARY

altricial: Born blind, naked, and dependent. Time is required before an altricial bird can fly and feed on its own. (See precocial)

anting: Birds' behavior of putting crushed or live ants in their feathers, supposedly to rid themselves of lice and mites. Over two hundred species of birds do this. Birds will also practice anting with substitute materials, even mothballs!

blind: Refers to a place where birders hide themselves when observing birds. Your house, car, tent, etc., can serve this function, allowing you to watch bird activities without their being aware of your presence.

breeding plumage (also called alternate plumage): The plumage, assumed by the males of some species, that functions to attract a mate. This plumage is usually more colorful than nonbreeding plumage. In the case of Starlings, both the male and female develop breeding plumage.

breeding season: The time of year during which a species nests and raises its young, usually the spring.

brood: The birds hatched from a single clutch of eggs. Many species will have two to three broods a year, depending upon the availability of resources.

brooding: Refers to the process whereby an adult bird will cover the nestlings with its body to protect them from heat, cold, or predators.

cache: To store food for later use. Birds will hide food in crevices, under leaves, and in soft ground. Species that cache food usually have a good memory for relocating it.

call: The brief and relatively simple sounds made by both male and female to maintain their pair bond or to sound an alarm. The young also make begging calls and location calls so the parents can find them.

cavity nester: A bird species that uses a cavity for nesting. There are primary cavity nesters, which actually create their own cavities, and secondary cavity nesters, which either use the cavities made by other birds or use natural cavities.

clutch: The set of eggs laid during a single nesting.

cooperative breeding: An arrangement in which birds not only live and feed in year-round groups, but jointly incubate the eggs and feed the nestlings which are the offspring of one or two pairs. Those helping are called "helpers at the nest."

crepuscular: Active at dawn and dusk.

crest: A tuft of longer feathers on the head, held erect by the bird.

crop: The enlarged portion of a bird's esophagus used to temporarily store food before it is processed by the stomach. The crop is also used by the Pigeon family to produce "pigeon's milk."

display behavior: Various postures, movements, and vocalizations used by a bird for communication. The different displays depend on whether a bird is attempting to attract a mate (courtship display), scare off a predator (threat display), keep a flock together, beg for food, etc.

distraction display: In what is often referred to as a "broken wing" display, a parent bird will lure a potential predator away from the nest or young by pretending to have a broken wing. When the predator is lured far enough away, the adult flies off.

diurnal: Active during the day.

drumming: A resonating sound made by woodpeckers during breeding season. They move their bills quickly against a tree branch, fence post, telephone pole, or the like. Drumming is used to attract mates and mark territories.

family: Birds are organized into family groups; the members share certain structural characteristics. Many of the characteristics are visible, so learning a family resemblance can help you identify birds in the field. Some families are large, including one hundred or more members, and some families have only one type.

feral: Said of a bird or other animal that was at one time domesticated but has since returned to a more wild state.

field marks: Those visible characteristics that identify a bird and distinguish it from other birds that look similar.

fledging: Flying from the nest after acquiring the feathers needed to do so. The length of time a bird is in the nest before acquiring the necessary feathers to fledge depends on the species.

fledgling: A bird just leaving the nest. It may continue to show traces of down. Most fledglings remain dependent upon the parents for food for some time after fledging (the time varies by species).

flycatch: A foraging technique used by some bird species whereby a bird will fly from a perch to catch an insect in the air.

forage: To search for and acquire food.

gape: The fleshy area around the bill. The gape is more pronounced in a nestling and immediately after fledging and often is a brighter color at that time.

genus: A group of related species.

gorget: The iridescent feathers on the throat of a male hummingbird.

habitat: That area within a species' general range where it prefers to live, often defined by the vegetation that occurs there. There are birds referred to as habitat "generalists" and those referred to as habitat "specialists." The generalists are those that can live well in practically any habitat, since their nesting and food requirements are broad. The specialists are those that can live well only in very specific habitats due to more strict requirements.

host: A species that is parasitized by another bird. Most victims of brood parasitism are open-cup nesters, such as sparrows and warblers.

hover-hunt: To hover in the air while searching for prey. This technique is used by the American Kestrel, for example.

immature: A young bird that has not acquired adult plumage but is capable of taking care of itself. "Immature" usually refers to the first year of a bird's life.

immature plumage: The feathers a bird has after losing its down but before it resembles the adult, from first-fall to subsequent plumages. In some species, the immature birds go through a series of molts (referred to as first-spring, first-summer, and so on) before attaining adult plumage.

incubate: The process whereby one or both parents cover the eggs with their bodies to keep the eggs warm until they hatch. Many females develop a "brood patch" by removing feathers from the belly area, which allows additional heat to be transferred to the eggs. Most birds don't begin incubating until all the eggs are laid. Most of our birds lay one egg a day until the clutch is complete.

juvenile: A young bird that has fledged and is able to care for itself but has not yet completed its molt from nestling plumage.

migrant: A bird that stops over temporarily during migration in the spring (as it flies to its nesting area) and during fall (when it returns to its winter home).

mixed-species flocks: Flocks comprised of different species of birds that congregate for feeding purposes. The birds have similar food habits, and the safety-in-numbers theory applies. Mixed-species flocks usually form at the end of the breeding season, a time when birds begin to wander in search of food resources.

molt: A natural process whereby a bird periodically loses its feathers, usually two at a time, and grows new ones. A complete molt takes place after the breeding season (called a postnuptial molt). At other times there are partial molts: only some feathers are renewed. A prenuptial molt also occurs in birds that assume a different breeding plumage, in the late winter or early spring.

nest (brood) parasitism: The act of laying eggs in another bird's nest, leaving them for the other bird (host) to care for them. The Brown-headed Cowbird is an example in our area of a bird that commonly leaves its eggs in other birds' nests.

nestling: This term refers to a bird from the time it has hatched until it leaves the nest. Nestlings have fluffy down before feathers come in.

nocturnal: A bird that is active at night; this includes most owls.

nonbreeding plumage (also referred to as basic plumage): The plumage that a bird acquires when molting after breeding season. This plumage will last until the next breeding season for those birds that molt only once a year. Some birds acquire a different (usually more colorful) plumage before breeding.

nonbreeding season: The time of year when breeding does not occur, primarily fall and winter.

omnivore: A bird or animal that eats a vast variety of plant and animal foods, rather than one type of food only.

passerine: A general term that refers to perching birds, primarily including small songbirds. It also applies to any bird within the order called Passeriformes, such as Crows. All passerines have three toes directed forward and one facing backward, which allows them to grip a perch tightly.

pest species: Birds that, having invaded an area or been introduced into it, compete with native species for food and nesting sites.

pigeon's milk: A secretion produced from the crop of both sexes in the Pigeon family. The "milk" is extremely nutritious and contains more protein and fat than human or cow milk. The young are fed on the pigeon's milk exclusively for the first few days after hatching.

plumage: The collective feathers of a bird.

precocial: Born feathered and capable of leaving the nest immediately. A precocial bird feeds on its own within a day. For example, Killdeer young are born precocial.

preen: The vital function of maintaining feathers by removing dirt and parasites living in them. Moving their feathers through their bills one at a time, birds work fresh oil into them from the oil gland at the base of their tails. They often preen after bathing.

range: The larger (total) area that a species is known to normally occur in at a given time of the year. If a bird is migratory, its range is divided into the breeding range and the wintering range.

raptors: Birds of prey (meat eating birds): hawks, eagles, falcons, and owls, primarily.

resident: A species that occurs year-round in a particular area.

riparian: Relating to, or living on, or located on the bank of a natural watercourse, such as a river. Sometimes also applied to lakes and tidewaters.

roost: To perch during the day to rest, or at night to sleep. Sometimes birds roost in large flocks, other times as family units or singly.

scientific name: The Latin name used to classify a plant or animal. Unlike a common name, which may apply to different species depending on your locale, a scientific name ensures that people are referring to the same species. The scientific name, often italicized, has two parts: the first is the genus and the second is the species.

semicolonial nesters: Birds that nest in loose groups, rather than separately.

song: Sounds used almost exclusively by males, although the females of a few species also sing. A male bird's song functions to advertise for a mate and to warn other males of the same species to stay out of his territory. A song may be complex or relatively simple. Birds sing much more during the spring and early summer, the breeding season.

species: A biological classification for individuals having common attributes and designated by the same name (American Robin, Western Bluebird, etc.). Even though two species may look very similar, they have different signals and behaviors that normally keep them from interbreeding and producing fertile offspring.

suet: A dense beef fat that provides high-energy food for birds, especially helpful in winter.

synchronous: Refers to an activity that is done all at the same time, rather than over the course of several days or weeks. For example, "synchronous hatching" refers to all the eggs in a nest hatching at the same time; "synchronous breeding" refers to birds of the same species in the same area breeding at the same time.

talons: The long, sharp claws on a raptor's foot, used for capturing prey.

taxonomy: The science of classifying plants and animals, including birds, by sorting them into groups with similar characteristics, then naming and describing the groups. Birds are grouped into order (sometimes suborder), family (sometimes subfamily), genus, and species (sometimes subspecies).

territory: That area defended aggressively by a bird. This varies greatly by time of year and by species. Some species defend only around their nests, some defend a much larger area during the breeding season, and some defend their feeding areas.

undertail coverts: The feathers that come down under the belly and meet where the tail attaches; not a part of the tail.

visitor: Species that occur in an area only during certain times of year; in the Inland Empire there are winter visitors and breeding visitors.

winter plumage: The males of some bird species assume different plumages in the winter and during breeding season. The winter plumage is paler and duller than normal. Both sexes of the European Starling also have a distinct winter plumage.

INDEX
TO BIRDS IN THIS BOOK

HEYDAY INSTITUTE

Since its founding in 1974, Heyday Books has occupied a unique niche in the publishing world, specializing in books that foster an understanding of the history, literature, art, environment, social issues, and culture of California and the West. We are a 501(c)(3) nonprofit organization based in Berkeley, California, serving a wide range of people and audiences.

We are grateful for the generous funding we've received for our publications and programs during the past year from foundations and more than three hundred and fifty individual donors. Major supporters include:

Anonymous; Audubon California; Judith and Phillip Auth; Barona Band of Mission Indians; B.C.W. Trust III; S. D. Bechtel, Jr. Foundation; Barbara and Fred Berensmeier; Berkeley Civic Arts Program and Civic Arts Commission; Joan Berman; Book Club of California; Peter and Mimi Buckley; Buena Vista Rancheria; Lewis and Sheana Butler; Butler Koshland Fund; California State Automobile Association; California State Coastal Conservancy; California State Library; Joanne Campbell; Candelaria Fund; John and Nancy Cassidy Family Foundation, through Silicon Valley Community Foundation; Creative Work Fund; Columbia Foundation; Colusa Indian Community Council; The Community Action Fund; Community Futures Collective; Compton Foundation, Inc.; Lawrence Crooks; Ida Rae Egli; Donald and Janice Elliott, in honor of David Elliott, through Silicon Valley Community Foundation; Evergreen Foundation; Federated Indians of Graton Rancheria; George Gamble; Wallace Alexander Gerbode Foundation; Richard & Rhoda Goldman Fund; Ben Graber, in honor of Sandy Graber; Evelyn & Walter Haas, Jr. Fund; Walter & Elise Haas Fund; James and Coke Hallowell; Cheryl Hinton; James Irvine Foundation; Mehdi Kashef; Marty and Pamela Krasney; LEF Foundation; Michael McCone; Morongo Band of Mission Indians; National Endowment for the Arts; National Park Service; Organize Training Center; Patagonia; Pease Family Fund, in honor of Bruce Kelley; Resources Legacy Fund; Robinson Rancheria Citizens Council; Alan Rosenus; San Francisco Foundation; San Manuel Band of Mission Indians; Deborah Sanchez; William Saroyan Foundation; Contee and Maggie Seely; Sandy Shapero; Jim Swinerton; Swinerton Family Fund; Taproot Foundation; Thendara Foundation; Marion Weber; Albert and Susan Wells; Peter Booth Wiley; Dean Witter Foundation; and Yocha Dehe Wintun Nation.

For more information about Heyday Institute, our publications and programs, please visit our website at www.heydaybooks.com.

RIVERSIDE-CORONA RESOURCE CONSERVATION DISTRICT

The Riverside-Corona Resource Conservation District (RCRCD) is a local government agency that works to conserve the natural resources (soil, water, plants, and wildlife) of parts of western Riverside and San Bernardino Counties in southern California. RCRCD provides educational programs for the community, technical guidance for land users, and conducts on-the-land conservation projects.

RCRCD fosters the sustainable use of resources in all land uses, including native habitats, urban areas, and agriculture through a variety of programs. For example:

- Resource Educators provide programs and pamphlets about methods to keep storm water clean, to manage landscapes, to control erosion, and more.

- An Irrigation Mobile Lab team evaluates watering systems to help landowners conserve water.

- Biologists rehabilitate degraded habitats by removing invasive plants and animals and restoring native species to natural landscapes.

- The District preserves important lands for wildlife corridors and to help maintain healthy ecosystems.

RCRCD hopes to empower people to steward their resources and to reduce their impacts on native species and landscapes. Thus this guide, with information about creating habitat-friendly yards that provide food, shelter, and water for birds and urban-adapted wildlife.

For more information about District programs, please see http://www.RCRCD.com.

INLANDIA
INSTITUTE

Inlandia Institute is a lively center of literary activity with offices in Riverside, California. It grew out of the highly acclaimed anthology *Inlandia: A Literary Journey through California's Inland Empire*, published by Heyday Books in 2006.

Inlandia Institute strives to nurture the rich and ongoing literary traditions of the region. Its mission is to recognize, support, and expand literary activity in all of its forms in inland Southern California by publishing books and sponsoring programs that deepen people's awareness, understanding, and appreciation of this unique, complex, and creatively vibrant area.

For more information about Inlandia Institute titles and programs please visit www.heydaybooks.com/imprints/inlandia-institute or http://www.inlandiainstitute.org.

ABOUT THE AUTHOR

Sheila Kee has been fascinated by everyday birds since she earned her Girl Scout "Bird Badge" in 1957. For ten years, she was a birder in western Riverside and San Bernardino Counties. She has been active in the San Bernardino Valley Audubon Society, serving as a board member and program chair. After retiring in 2005, she and her husband moved to the Pacific Northwest, where she continues to pursue her birding interests.

Sheila was a staff research associate for the University of California Cooperative Extension at Riverside for fifteen years. She holds a Master of Community Planning from the University of Maryland and a Bachelor of Science in wildlife management from Humboldt State University.

The first edition of *Backyard Birds of the Inland Empire* won the 2002 District Outreach Award for Special Publications (sponsored by the National Association of Conservation Districts and the Association of Equipment Manufacturers).

Be forewarned: Sheila's enthusiasm for birds is infectious.

Self-portrait by Sheila Kee